Grammar Practice Workbook

GRADE 3

Requests for permission to make copies of any part of the work should be submitted through our Permissions website at https://customercare.hmhco.com/contactus/Permissions.html or mailed to Houghton Mifflin Harcourt Publishing Company, Attn: Rights Compliance and Analysis, 9400 Southpark Center Loop, Orlando, Florida 32819-8647.

Printed in the U.S.A.

ISBN 978-0-358-24500-1

1 2 3 4 5 6 7 8 9 10   0928   28 27 26 25 24 23 22 21 20 19

4500768328   A B C D E F G

Grade 3

Contents

The Subject of a Simple Sentence

A **sentence** is a group of words that tells a complete thought. The **subject** of a simple sentence tells whom or what the sentence is about.

The subject can be one word or more than one word. The **complete subject** includes all the words in the subject.

My grandmother was born in Michigan.

A **simple subject** has a single subject that completes the action in a sentence. A **compound subject** have two or more subjects joined by a **coordinating conjunction**.

My brother *and* his friend went to the movie theater.

▷ **Write the complete subject of each simple sentence. Identify whether the subject is simple or compound.**

1. Saturday is my birthday. _____ MY _____

2. My cousins and their parents live in New Jersey. My cousins and Parer

3. The snow in the mountains was melting. the snow

4. My teacher and I like jazz. My teacher and I

5. Louise and her puppy live a block away from me. Louise and her Puppy

6. The red notebook fell off the desk. the red notebook

7. Mint chocolate chip and vanilla are my favorite ice cream flavors.
MY

8. Max and his brother go to college in Maine. Max and his brother

9. I really love science fiction movies. I really love sci fi

10. The kittens and their mother rolled around on the floor.
the kittens and their mother

▷ **Revisit your piece of writing. Edit the draft to make sure all subjects in a simple sentence are used correctly.**

The Predicate of a Simple Sentence

Every simple sentence has two parts—the subject and the predicate.

The **predicate** is the part of a sentence that tells what the **subject** does or is.

Matt <u>rides</u> his bike. A **compound predicate** has two or more actions joined by a **coordinating conjunction**. My cat <u>runs and plays</u> all day.

The **simple predicate** is the verb that shows the action. The complete predicate includes all the words in the predicate.

▶ **Write each simple predicate. Then underline the complete predicate. If the sentence contains a compound predicate, write "compound."**

1. Kyle eats a juicy apple. _____

2. I sit and read under the tree. _____

3. Loretta swims in the lake. _____

4. My old dog sleeps all afternoon. _____

5. Yvette painted and framed her favorite picture. _____

▶ **Revisit your piece of writing. Edit the draft to make sure all predicates in a simple sentence are used correctly.**

Name **nateo D'ambrosio**

Sentence Fragments

A **sentence** is a group of words that tells a complete thought. It tells who or what, and it tells an action or state of being. A sentence that is not a complete thought is called a **fragment**.

Sentence: A woman drove her car to the grocery store.

Fragment: drove her car

> **Write the group of words that will complete each sentence.**

1. The robin ___looked for worms.___
   looked for worms   on the fence

2. Alexander ___jokes___.
   funny   is good at telling jokes

3. ___Johanna___ takes tap dance lessons.
   ran away   Johanna

4. ___Two small frogs___ jumped to a lily pad.
   Two small frogs   hopped along

5. Mrs. Tartt ___drove us home from school___
   kind   drove us home from school

> **Revisit your piece of writing. Edit the draft to make sure all subjects in a simple sentence are used correctly.**

Review Simple Sentences

▶ **Write the complete subject of each simple sentence. Then underline the complete predicate.**

1. My best friend and I like to play video games.

   _____

2. The movie had already started by the time we got there.

   _____

3. Our dog Fancy loves to swim in the lake.

   _____

4. The band concert was postponed because of the snowstorm.

   _____

5. Eddie and his sister Leah looked for hermit crabs in the sand.

   _____

▶ **Revisit your piece of writing. Edit the draft to make sure all simple sentences are written correctly.**

Connect to Writing: Using Simple Sentences

> **Read the selection and choose the best answer to each question.**

Read the following paragraph about a girl and her cat. Look for any revisions that should be made. Then answer the questions that follow.

(1) Rhonda has a cat. (2) Loves to eat fish treats. (3) The cat has a toy mouse. (4) He likes to chase it around the living room. (5) This makes Rhonda laugh. (6) Her cat also sleeps a lot. (7) The cat her lap. (8) He purrs when he sleeps.

1. 1. Which of the following is not a complete sentence?

   A. Rhonda has a cat.

   B. Loves to eat fish treats.

   C. The cat has a toy mouse.

   D. He likes to chase it around the living room.

2. Which of the following is not a complete sentence?

   A. This makes Rhonda laugh.

   B. Her cat also sleeps a lot.

   C. The cat her lap.

   D. He purrs when he sleeps.

> **Do you have a pet? If not, what kind of pet would you like? Write two or three sentences about your pet or one you would like to have.**

_____

_____

_____

Statements and Questions

A sentence that tells something is a **statement**. It ends with a period. It is also called a declarative sentence.

A sentence that asks something is a **question**. It ends with a question mark. It is also called an interrogative sentence.

Statement/Declarative	Question/Interrogative
I live on Chestnut Street.	Where do you live?

▶ Write *statement* if the sentence tells something. Write *question* if the sentence asks something.

1. How many pages do you have left to read? _Question_

2. Who is coming to Rose's party? _Queston_

3. I saw a wonderful painting at the museum. _Statment_

4. There are three kinds of beans in this salad. _Statement_

5. Ancient Romans cooked with olive oil. _Statment_

6. Where is my new bracelet? _Question_

7. Uncle Randy is a great storyteller. _Statment_

8. What time is the baseball game? _Question_

9. Will it rain tomorrow? _Question_

10. We stayed in a cabin in the mountains. _Statment_

▶ Revisit your piece of writing. Edit the draft to make sure all statements and questions are used correctly.

Name _____

Commands and Exclamations

A **command** is a sentence that tells someone to do something. It ends with a period. It is also called an imperative sentence.

An **exclamation** is a sentence that shows strong feeling, such as excitement, surprise, or fear. It ends with an exclamation point. It is also called an exclamatory sentence.

Command/Imperative
Please do the dishes.

Exclamation/Exclamatory
Don't go too far!

> Write *command* if the sentence tells someone to do something. Write *exclamation* if the sentence shows strong feeling.

1. Don't wake the sleeping baby. _command_

2. Please help me fold the laundry. _command_

3. Get away from that snake! _Exclamation_

4. I can't believe you threw a surprise party for me! _Exclamation_

5. Go in the side door. _command_

> Revisit your piece of writing. Edit the draft to make sure all commands and exclamations are used correctly.

Statements, Questions, Commands, and Exclamations

▶ Write *statement* if the sentence tells something. Write *question* if the sentence asks something.

1. Susanna takes ballet lessons on Fridays. _Statement_

2. What is your favorite thing to do after school? _question_

3. How long do these cookies need to go in the oven? _question_

4. Roger and I have been friends since kindergarten. _statment_

5. My grandmother made me a quilt for my bed. _statment_

▶ Write *command* if the sentence tells someone to do something. Write *exclamation* if the sentence shows strong feeling.

6. That essay you wrote was amazing! _exclamation_

7. Please take the garbage outside. _____

8. I can't believe Jackie caught the ball! _____

9. What a great new dress you're wearing! _____

10. Don't stir the batter too much. _____

▶ Revisit your piece of writing. Edit the draft to make sure all question types are used correctly.

Review Kinds of Sentences

There are four kinds of sentences.

Mom is home.	**Declarative** (statement)
Did you study?	**Interrogative** (question)
Pick up that mess.	**Imperative** (command)
What a great job!	**Exclamatory** (exclamation)

▶ Write *statement* if the sentence tells something. Write *question* if the sentence asks something. Write *command* if the sentence tells someone to do something. Write *exclamation* if the sentence shows strong feeling.

1. That was the best movie I ever saw! _exclamation_

2. Alex and Malik are only two months apart. _statement_

3. This is the oldest house on the block. _statement_

4. Please wipe your feet on the mat. _command_

5. Do you like to swim? _question_

6. I was so surprised to see Lisa there! _exclamation_

7. What are you doing next Thursday? _question_

8. Come back in a half hour. _command_

9. The goat jumped over the fence. _statement_

10. Where is my writing journal? _question_

▶ Revisit your piece of writing. Edit the draft to make sure all sentence types are used correctly.

Connect to Writing: Using Different Kinds of Sentences

> **Read the selection and choose the best answer to each question.**

Read the following paragraph about a robot competition. Look for any revisions that should be made. Then answer the questions that follow.

(1) My friend Julie and I entered a robot competition. (2) We worked really hard on our robot? (3) After three weeks, our robot was complete. (4) It was able to walk a short distance. (5) But would we win a prize. (6) We did! (7) We won third prize! (8) Our hard work had paid off.

1. Which of the following sentences has the wrong punctuation?

   A. My friend Julie and I entered a robot competition.

   B. We worked really hard on our robot?

   C. After three weeks, our robot was complete.

   D. It was able to walk a short distance.

2. Which of the following sentences has the wrong punctuation?

   A. But would we win a prize.

   B. We did!

   C. We won third prize!

   D. Our hard work had paid off.

> **If you could build a robot, what would you want it to do? Write two or three sentences about it.**

1. I will make it have Powers.
2. I I will call it Goku

Simple and Compound Sentences

and
or
but
so

A **simple sentence** tells a complete thought with a subject and verb that agree.

A **compound sentence** is made up of two simple sentences joined by the word *and, but, or,* or *so.*

> We went for ice cream after dinner. Our cousins came, too.

> We went for ice cream after dinner, <u>and</u> our cousins came, too.

▶ **Determine whether each sentence is simple or compound. Write simple or compound on the line.**

1. He didn't want to go to the eye doctor, but he went anyway.

   compound

2. A cactus is a type of plant that can live in dry climates.

   simple

3. Everyone was busy, so I watched TV alone.

   compound

4. Do you want to play a game, or would you rather watch a movie?

   compound

5. My best friend Harry will only write with green pens.

   simple

▶ **Revisit your piece of writing. Edit the draft to make sure all simple and compound sentences are used correctly.**

Coordinating Conjunctions

A **compound sentence** is made up of two simple sentences joined by a **conjunction** such as *and, but, or*, and *so*. A comma comes before the conjunction.

And joins two similar ideas.   *But* joins two different ideas.

Or joins two possible ideas.

So shows that the second idea happens because of the first.

▸ **Write the conjunction that best joins the simple sentences. Then write the compound sentence.**

1. Gina wrote to Betsy. She wrote to Erin.

   _____

2. Daniel was at the pool. Miriam was not at the pool.

   _____

3. I know you're tired. I will let you rest.

   _____

4. Tony likes almonds. He does not like peanuts.

   _____

5. Felicity's family will be out of town. She will not go to the party.

   _____

▸ **Revisit your piece of writing. Edit the draft to make sure all coordinating conjunctions are used correctly.**

Run-On Sentences

Two or more simple sentences that run together are called run-on sentences.

A run-on sentence may be corrected by forming a compound sentence. The conjunctions *and, but, or,* and *so* are used to form compound sentences.

Lauren does not have a sister Maxim does.

Lauren does not have a sister, <u>but</u> Maxim does.

▷ **Correct each run-on sentence by forming a compound sentence. Write the conjunction and then write the compound sentence.**

1. My aunt does not eat meat she does not eat eggs.

   _____

2. Samantha can make toast she cannot make pancakes.

   _____

3. Do you like the winter do you prefer the summer?

   _____

4. My cat likes sleeping on the couch he likes sleeping on my bed more.

   _____

5. Will you leave now will you stay longer?

   _____

▷ **Revisit your piece of writing. Edit the draft to make sure all run-on sentences are corrected.**

Review Compound Sentences

A **compound sentence** is made up of two simple sentences joined by a comma followed by a **conjunction**. The words *and, but, or,* and *so* are conjunctions. Two simple sentences that run together without using a comma and a conjunction are called a run-on sentence.

Nina will go to the concert she will go to the movies.

Nina will go to the concert, <u>or</u> she will go to the movies.

▶ **Write the conjunction that best joins the two simple sentences into one compound sentence. Then write the compound sentence.**

1. The frogs croak all day. They are quiet at night.

_____

2. I can't remember the address. I will have to look it up.

_____

▶ **Correct the run-on sentence by using a comma and a conjunction to form a compound sentence.**

3. Riding a bike is fun I like hiking better.

_____

4. Naomi is my best friend she is also my cousin.

_____

5. It is raining we will play basketball in the gym.

_____

▶ **Revisit your piece of writing. Edit the draft to make sure all compound sentences are used correctly.**

Connect to Writing: Using Compound Sentences

> **Read the selection and choose the best answer to each question.**

Read the following paragraph about a new friend. Look for any revisions that should be made. Then answer the questions that follow.

(1) Victoria loves music, but she is learning to play the piano. (2) She takes lessons once a week with Mr. Wade, and she practices at home. (3) One day, she forgot her music book. (4) Mr. Wade asked her to play what she remembered. (5) Somehow, she was able to play the whole piece from memory. (6) Mr. Wade was pleased, so he asked her to bring her music next time.

1. What change should be made to sentence 1?

   A. Change *but* to *if*.

   B. Change *but* to *yet*.

   C. Change *but* to *and*.

   D. Make no change.

2. What change should be made to sentence 6?

   A. Change *so* to *but*.

   B. Change *so* to *and*.

   C. Change *so* to *or*.

   D. Make no change.

> **What musical instrument would you like to play? Write two or three sentences about it.**

_____

_____

_____

Subject-Verb Agreement

A verb that tells about an action that is happening now is in the present tense. Verbs in the present tense have two forms. The correct form to use depends on the subject of the sentence.

Except for *I*, add –*s* to the verb when the noun in the subject is singular. Do not add –*s* to the verb when the noun in the subject is plural.

My dog Pepper barks at the dogs next door.

The dogs next door bark when they see Pepper coming.

> **Underline the correct present-tense verb in parentheses. Then write each sentence correctly.**

1. People (walk, walks) along the boardwalk at night.

pearle walk along the board walk at night.

2. Andrew (write, writes) to his sister in college.

andrew writes to his sister in college.

3. I (love, loves) banana splits with whipped cream.

I love banana spits with whipped cream.

4. The cats (eat, eats) all the food in the bowl.

the cats eat all the food in the bowl.

5. The hawk (land, lands) on the highest branch.

the hawk lands on the highest branch

> **Revisit your piece of writing. Edit the draft to make sure all subject-verb agreement is used correctly.**

Adding –s or –es to Verbs

Some verbs end with –es instead of –s. Add –es to verbs that end with s, sh, ch, or x when they are used with a singular noun in the subject. Do not add –es when the noun in the subject is plural.

Some verbs end with a consonant and y. Change the y to i, and add –es when you use this kind of verb with a singular noun.

The boy <u>reaches</u> for another cookie.

Greta <u>hurries</u> to catch the bus.

The verb *reach* adds –es. The verb hurry changes the y to i and adds –es.

▶ **Underline the correct present-tense verb in parentheses. Then write each sentence correctly.**

1. Helena (asks, askes) her sister for help with her math homework.

   helen askes her sister whith her math homework.

2. Nate's dog (watchs, watches) him through the window.

   nates dog watches him through the window

3. Kathryn (worrys, worries) that she will be late to school.

   kathryn worrys that she will be late to school.

4. Nigel (rushs, rushes) to be first in line.

   nige rushe tobe first in line.

5. Mr. Singh (fixs, fixes) the wheel on Ina's scooter.

   mr. Singh fixes wheel on Ina scooter.

▶ **Revisit your piece of writing. Edit the draft to make sure all verbs are written correctly.**

_____

Singular and Plural Subjects

▶ **Write the correct form of the verb in parentheses to complete each sentence.**

1. Debbie ___washes___ her dog in the bathtub. (wash)

2. Joshua ___mixes___ the cake batter. (mix)

3. I ___watch___ my cat play with her toy mouse. (watch)

4. Frankie and her brother ___bakes___ brownies after school. (bake)

5. Tim ___brushes___ the horse after he rides her. (brush)

6. Holden ___waits___ for his name to be called. (wait)

7. My dad ___coaches___ our Little League team. (coach)

8. Raquel and I ___walk___ along the seashore. (walk)

9. Mia ___catches___ the ball thrown to her. (catch)

10. The bus ___carrys___ passengers into the amusement park. (carry)

▶ **Revisit your piece of writing. Edit the draft to make sure all singular and plural subjects are used correctly.** _____

Review Subject-Verb Agreement

> Verbs in the present tense have two forms. The correct form to use depends on the subject of the sentence.
>
> Except for *I*, add −*s* to the verb when the noun in the subject is singular. Do not add −*s* to the verb when the noun in the subject is plural.
>
> Add −*es* to verbs that end with *s*, *sh*, *ch*, or *x* when they are used with a singular noun in the subject. Do not add −*es* when the noun in the subject is plural.
>
> Some verbs end with a consonant and *y*. Change the *y* to *i*, and add −*es* when you use this kind of verb with a singular noun.

▶ **Underline the correct present-tense verb in parentheses. Then write each sentence correctly.**

1. Julia and I (carry, carries) the huge box across the room.

   Julia and I carry the huge box across the room

2. I (love, loves) sandwiches made with strawberry jam.

   I love sandwiches made with strawberry jam

3. Sarah (run, runs) every morning with the track team.

   sarah runs every morning with the track team

4. Luis (sing, sings) in the middle school chorus.

   luis sings in the middle school chorus.

5. My dog Patience (try, tries) to sneak food from the table.

   My dog Patience try to sneak food from the table.

▶ **Revisit your piece of writing. Edit the draft to make sure all subject-verb agreement is used correctly.**

Connect to Writing: Using Correct Subject-Verb Agreement

> Read the selection and choose the best answer to each question.

Read the following paragraph about Komodo dragons. Look for any revisions that should be made. Then answer the questions that follow.

(1) The largest lizard in the world is the Komodo dragon. (2) Komodo dragons lives on four islands of Indonesia. (3) They use their tongue in order to find prey by smell. (4) Komodo dragons weighs up to 200 pounds. (5) They can run up to 13 miles an hour.

1. What change should be made to sentence 2?

   A. Change *lives* to *live*.

   B. Change *islands* to *island*.

   C. Change *Komodo* to *Komodos*.

   D. Make no change.

2. What change should be made to sentence 4?

   A. Change *pounds* to *pound*.

   B. Change *dragons* to *dragon*.

   C. Change *weighs* to *weigh*.

   D. Make no change.

> **What is an animal that you would like to learn more about? Write two or three sentences about what you would like to learn.**

_____

_____

_____

Pronoun-Verb Agreement

> **Verbs** show action in sentences and tell when that action happens. Verbs that tell about actions that are happening now are in the present tense.
>
> You add –s or –es to the verb when the pronoun in the subject *is he, she,* or *it.*
>
> You do not add –s or –es to the verb when the pronoun in the subject is *I, you, we,* or *they.*
>
>   He <u>runs</u> very fast.
>
>   They <u>run</u> even faster.

> **Underline the present-tense verb in parentheses that agrees with the subject pronoun. Then write each sentence correctly.**

1. She (walk, walks) past the train tracks.

   _____

2. They (laugh, laughs) at my silly jokes.

   _____

3. I (write, writes) stories set in the future.

   _____

4. We (eat, eats) dinner at six o'clock.

   _____

5. Nakomo (ride, rides) his bike to school.

   _____

> **Revisit your piece of writing. Edit the draft to make sure all pronoun-verb agreement is used correctly.**

When to Add –*es* or –*ies*

> Most verbs in the present end with *s* when the pronoun in the subject is *he, she,* or *it*. Add –*es* to verbs that end in *s, sh, ch,* or *x*.
>
> Do not add –*s* or –*es* to verbs when the pronoun in the subject is *I, you, we,* or *they*.
>
> Some verbs end with a consonant and *y*. Change the *y* to *i* and add –*es* when the pronoun in the subject is *he, she,* or *it*.
>
> You do not change the *y* to *i* and add –*es* when the pronoun in the subject is *I, you, we,* or *they*.

▶ **Underline the present-tense verb in parentheses that agrees with the subject pronoun. Then write each sentence correctly.**

1. I (march, marches) with the band in the July 4th parade.

_____

2. He (hurry, hurries) out the door with his backpack.

_____

3. She (catch, catches) the ball with her left hand.

_____

4. We (mix, mixes) the colors before we start painting.

_____

5. Ekene (crush, crushes) aluminum cans before putting them in the recycling bin.

_____

▶ **Revisit your piece of writing. Edit the draft to make sure all verbs are used correctly.**

Pronoun-Verb Agreement

▶ **Write the present-tense form of the verb in parentheses that agrees with the subject pronoun.**

1. They _____ on the project all weekend. (work)

2. On Saturdays we _____ our grandmother. (visit)

3. He _____ Spanish in school. (study)

4. She _____ her little brother on the swing. (push)

5. They _____ their dog in the bathtub. (wash)

6. We _____ brownies for the class party. (bake)

7. You _____ when I sing in a silly voice. (laugh)

8. They _____ to get in line. (rush)

9. I _____ all my books back to the library. (carry)

10. She _____ the flour into the other ingredients. (mix)

▶ **Revisit your piece of writing. Edit the draft to make sure all pronoun-verb agreement is used correctly.**

Review Pronoun-Verb Agreement

Most verbs in the present end with −s when the pronoun in the subject is *he, she,* or *it.*

Add −es to verbs that end in *s, sh, ch,* or *x.*

You do not add −s or −es to the verb when the pronoun in the subject is *I, you, we,* or *they.*

Some verbs end with a consonant and *y.* Change the *y* to *i* and add −es when the pronoun in the subject is *he, she,* or *it.*

You do not change the *y* to *i* and add −es when the pronoun in the subject is *I, you, we,* or *they.*

▷ **Write the present-tense form of the verb in parentheses that agrees with the subject pronoun.**

1. It ___climbes___ onto the branch above us. (climb) ✓

2. They ___read___ science fiction books. (read) ✓

3. We ___try___ to feed our dog at the same time every day. (try) ✓

4. She ___copyes___ the drawing from a comic book. (copy) ✓

5. He ___weares___ red sneakers every day. (wear) ✓

▷ **Revisit your piece of writing. Edit the draft to make sure all pronoun-verb agreement is used correctly.**

Connect to Writing: Using Correct Pronoun-Verb Agreement

> **Read the selection and choose the best answer to each question.**

Read the following paragraph about a boy who walks fast. Look for any revisions that should be made. Then answer the questions that follow.

(1) My friend Haruki is a very fast walker. (2) Every day, we hurry to catch up with him. (3) He does not even notice how fast he is going. (4) Then he look behind him. (5) We are all so far behind. (6) He promises to slow down. (7) But then he is off again!

1. What change should be made to sentence 2?

   A. Change *hurry* to *hurries*.

   B. Change *hurry* to *hurrys*.

   C. Change *hurry* to *hurryes*.

   D. Make no change.

2. What change should be made to sentence 4?

   A. Change *look* to *lookes*.

   B. Change *look* to *looks*.

   C. Change *look* to *lookies*.

   D. Make no change.

> **How do you walk? Are you fast or slow? Write two or three sentences about it.**

_____

_____

_____

Complex Sentences

An **independent clause** is a simple sentence and tells a complete thought. It has a subject and a verb.

A **dependent clause** has a subject and a verb, but it does not tell a complete thought.

A **complex sentence** is formed by combining one independent clause and one or more dependent clauses.

> Although it was raining. We went out for a walk.

> Although it was raining, we went out for a walk.

▶ Write *complex* if the sentence has an independent clause and one or more dependent clauses. Write *dependent clause* if the sentence does not tell a complete thought.

1. When we opened the door, our dog rushed out of the house. _____

2. While the deer stopped to eat grass. _____

3. Before I arrived in New York. _____

4. As Lindsey read her book, she ate one raisin per page. _____

5. Because of a landslide, the road was closed. _____

▶ Revisit your piece of writing. Edit the draft to make sure all dependent and independent clauses are used correctly.

Subordinating Conjunctions

A **complex sentence** is formed by combining one independent clause and at least one dependent clause. If the dependent clause appears first, add a comma after it.

Subordinating conjunctions begin dependent clauses. Some subordinating conjunctions are *after, although, because, before, even though, since, unless, until, when,* and *while.*

Justin and Grace were sad. Because it was too cold to swim.

Justin and Grace were sad <u>because</u> it was too cold to swim.

▶ **Underline the dependent clause. Write the subordinating conjunction that begins the dependent clause.**

1. After we got home that night, it started to snow. _____

2. I am going to learn badminton this summer because we are getting a set.

_____

3. Ricky was angry at his brother for breaking his cup even though it was an

accident. _____

4. June will stir the oatmeal while you add in the banana slices.

_____

5. Unless I clean my room, my mom won't let me go to the skate park

Saturday. _____

▶ **Revisit your piece of writing. Edit the draft to make sure all subordinating conjunctions are used correctly.**

Forming Complex Sentences

> A **complex sentence** is formed by combining one independent clause and one or more dependent clauses.
>
> Once she gets home from work, Kirsten can help you with your math.
>
> Kirsten can help you with your math once she gets home from work.

> **Combine the clauses to form complex sentences.**

1. Even though Max loves chocolate cake. He does not like plain chocolate.

_____

2. We stayed at the ball game. Until it started to rain.

_____

3. Because the play had ended. They stood up in their seats.

_____

4. After I get home. We can play some games together.

_____

5. My dog hid in the bathtub. Before the storm even started.

_____

> **Revisit your piece of writing. Edit the draft to make sure all complex sentences are formed correctly.**

Review Complex Sentences

A **complex sentence** is formed by combining one independent clause and one or more dependent clauses. If the dependent clause appears first, add a comma after it.

Subordinating conjunctions begin dependent clauses. Some subordinating conjunctions are *after, although, because, before, even though, since, unless, until, when,* and *while.*

▶ **Combine the clauses to form complex sentences.**

1. After the storm was over. Kareem saw large branches on the ground.

   _____

2. When Danica finally dove off the high diving board. Everyone cheered.

   _____

3. I love broccoli now. Because we roasted it in the oven.

   _____

4. Since winter is coming. It is time to get my heavy coat out.

   _____

5. We had to leave early in the morning. Even though it was still dark.

   _____

▶ **Revisit your piece of writing. Edit the draft to make sure all complex sentences are used correctly.**

Connect to Writing: Using Complex Sentences

> **Read the selection and choose the best answer to each question.**

Read the following paragraph about two friends who share fruit. Look for any revisions that should be made. Then answer the questions that follow.

(1) Kara shares her apples with me because she knows I love them. (2) When I visit my grandmother in Georgia. (3) I always bring back fresh fruit for Kara. (4) Peaches are her favorite. (5) After she bites into a peach, juice runs down her chin. (6) This always makes us laugh.

1. What is wrong with sentence 2?

   A. It is a complex sentence.

   B. It is a dependent clause.

   C. It is an independent clause.

   D. There is nothing wrong with sentence 2.

2. Which of the following is a complex sentence?

   A. I always bring back fresh fruit for Kara.

   B. Peaches are her favorite.

   C. After she bites into a peach, juice runs down her chin.

   D. This always makes us laugh.

> **What do you like to share with a friend? Write two or three sentences about it.**

_____

_____

_____

Identifying Nouns and Subjects

A word that names a person, a place, or a thing is a **noun**. The noun that is doing something in a sentence is the **subject**.

My **dad** loves to bake <u>bread</u>.

▷ **Write the two nouns in each sentence. Circle the subject of each sentence.**

1. The wind blew my scarf off. _____

2. Lesley takes ballet twice a week. _____

3. The rabbits hopped through the field. _____

4. Our group worked on a project together. _____

5. Phoebe spun around in a circle. _____

6. Ramon has three brothers. _____

7. The sun set behind the mountains. _____

8. My grandfather tends to his garden. _____

9. My sister has very curly hair. _____

10. Kyoko hiked through the woods. _____

▷ **Revisit your piece of writing. Edit the draft to make sure all nouns and subjects are used correctly.**

Capitalizing Nouns

A word that names a person, place, or thing is a **noun**.

Common nouns name any person, place, or thing. **Proper nouns** name a particular person, place, or thing.

Proper nouns begin with capital letters and may have more than one word. People's titles and important words in titles of books are capitalized. Holidays and geographical names and places are also capitalized.

My sister Catherine works at a company in Rochester.

My family visited the Grand Canyon over the Memorial Day weekend.

▷ **Write *common* or *proper* for each underlined noun.**

1. When we visited New York, we had great pizza. _____

2. Angela decided to get pepperoni on her pizza. _____

3. I don't like pepperoni, but I do like pineapple on pizza. _____

4. We also had a delicious dinner in Chinatown one night. _____

5. During the day, we visited the Empire State Building. _____

6. The first day of school is always the day after Labor Day. _____

▷ **Revisit your piece of writing. Edit the draft to make sure all proper nouns are capitalized correctly.**

Common and Proper Nouns

> **Write the two nouns in each sentence. Circle the noun that is the subject of the sentence.**

1. The children ran to see the elephants. _____

2. Courtney wore her new black dress. _____

3. The cat hid inside the closet. _____

4. Spinach is my favorite vegetable. _____

5. The cars were racing around the track. _____

> **Write _common_ or _proper_ for each underlined noun.**

6. We picked two quarts of <u>strawberries</u> in one hour. _____

7. My mother is very interested in the <u>Civil War</u>. _____

8. In the <u>spring</u>, Loraine will visit her cousins in California. _____

9. Kevin loves to go to the Museum of Science in <u>Boston</u>. _____

10. Jorge is visiting his grandmother for <u>Thanksgiving</u>. _____

> **Revisit your piece of writing. Edit the draft to make sure all common and proper nouns are used correctly.**

Review Common and Proper Nouns

A word that names a person, a place, or a thing is a **noun**.

Common nouns name any person, place, or thing. **Proper nouns** name a particular person, place, or thing.

Proper nouns begin with capital letters and may have more than one word. People's titles and important words in titles of books are capitalized.

▶ **Write common or proper for each underlined noun.**

1. When we went to California, we swam in the <u>Pacific Ocean</u>. _____

2. The last <u>movie</u> I saw was about a space colony on Mars. _____

3. Jackie threw pieces of <u>bread</u> to the ducks in Willow Pond. _____

▶ **Write the sentences correctly. Capitalize the appropriate underlined words.**

4. Last week, ms. whittier took us to the museum of art.

_____

5. I have always wanted to visit the grand canyon in arizona.

_____

▶ **Revisit your piece of writing. Edit the draft to make sure all nouns are used correctly.**

Connect to Writing: Using Common and Proper Nouns

▶ **Read the selection and choose the best answer to each question.**
Read the following paragraph about an airplane ride. Look for any revisions that should be made. Then answer the questions that follow.

(1) Last summer, my family took a trip to Florida. (2) I had never been on an Airplane before. (3) It was thrilling to look down and see everything from the air. (4) I already knew what I wanted to do as soon as we touched down. (5) I have wanted to go to everglades national park my whole life! (6) My parents told me I had to wait, but we'll be heading there in the morning.

1. What change should be made to sentence 2?

   A. The word *before* should be capitalized.

   B. The word *Airplane* should be lowercase.

   C. The word *I* should be lowercase.

   D. Make no change.

2. What change should be made to sentence 5?

   A. The words *whole life* should be capitalized.

   B. The words *everglades national park* should be capitalized.

   C. The word *wanted* should be capitalized.

   D. Make no change.

▶ **If you could travel on an airplane, where would you like to go? Write two or three sentences about it.**

_____

_____

_____

Name _____

Identifying Singular and Plural Nouns

A noun that names only one person, place, or thing is a **singular noun**. A noun that names more than one person, place, or thing is a **plural noun**. Add −s to most singular nouns to form the plural.

Nick played a <u>game</u> in his room.   Nick played <u>games</u> in his room.

They studied for their math <u>test</u>.   They studied for all their <u>tests</u>.

▷ Write *singular* or *plural* for each underlined noun.

1. Our <u>moms</u> will be upset if we stay out too late. _____

2. You did not give me credit for my great <u>idea</u>. _____

3. The <u>horses</u> in the barn all wore a blanket. _____

4. There are 30 days in the <u>month</u> of September. _____

5. The cat had five <u>kittens</u>. _____

▷ Write the plural form of the noun in parentheses to complete the sentence.

6. Please finish all the _____ on your plate. (pea)

7. I can't find my favorite cat _____ . (sock)

8. We heard some _____ hooting in the night. (owl)

9. Kendra has two _____ and one sister. (brother)

10. Six _____ were parked in front of the school. (truck)

▷ Revisit your piece of writing. Edit the draft to make sure all singular and plural nouns are used correctly.

Plural Nouns with –s

Add –s to most nouns to form the plural.			
Singular:	shirt	frog	ladder
Plural:	shirts	frogs	ladders

> Write the plural form of the underlined noun.

1. We saw a red bird on our lawn. Soon there were many red

   _____ at our bird feeder.

2. Minna cut out a picture from a magazine. Then she cut out more

   _____ to make a collage.

3. I grabbed an apple from the fruit bowl. There were only two

   _____ left.

4. Mike found an old photograph of his mother. She showed him more

   _____.

5. My favorite flower is a rose. But I do like lots of other _____.

> Revisit your piece of writing. Edit the draft to make sure all singular and plural nouns are used correctly.

Plural Nouns with –s and –es

Add –s to most nouns to form the plural.

Add –es to nouns that end in s, sh, ch, and x to form the plural.

Singular: chair   box   peach

Plural: chairs   boxes   peaches

▶ **Write the plural form of the noun in parentheses to complete the sentence.**

1. Please bring the water _____ to the table. (glass)

2. My mother pulled our _____ out of the attic. (suitcase)

3. I had to use two _____ before the candle would light. (match)

4. Our teacher separated us into two _____ for a math game. (group)

5. We will need your names and _____ for our records. (address)

▶ **Revisit your piece of writing. Edit the draft to make sure all plural nouns are used correctly.**

Review Plural Nouns with –s and –es

A noun that names only one person, place, or thing is a **singular noun**. A noun that names more than one person, place, or thing is a **plural noun**.

Add –s to most singular nouns to form the plural.

Add –es to nouns that end in s, sh, ch, and x to form the plural.

▸ **Write** *singular* **or** *plural* **for each underlined noun.**

1. This huge book has over 400 <u>pages</u>. _____

2. After her run, Jessie drank two <u>glasses</u> of water. _____

3. My brother and I surprised our mom with a <u>cake</u> for her birthday.

   _____

▸ **Write the plural form of the noun in parentheses to complete the sentence.**

4. I can't wait to open these _____ that came from my grandparents. (box)

5. Tony ate an entire bowl of _____. (peanut)

▸ **Revisit your piece of writing. Edit the draft to make sure all plural nouns are used correctly.**

Connect to Writing: Using Plural Nouns with –s and –es

> **Read the selection and choose the best answer to each question.**

Read the following paragraph about a boy looking for a lost book. Look for any revisions that should be made. Then answer the questions that follow.

(1) One day, Marshall went looking for his favorite book about dinosaurs. (2) It was not where he thought it would be. (3) First, he looked on all the shelves on his bookcase. (4) Then he went through the boxs in his closet. (5) He was about to give up, when he saw a book peeking out from under his bed. (6) Of course, it was his favorite dinosaur book!

1. What change should be made to sentence 3?

   A. Change *shelves* to *shelfs*.

   B. Change *shelves* to *shelfes*.

   C. Change *shelves* to *shelvs*.

   D. Make no change.

2. What change should be made to sentence 4?

   A. Change *boxs* to *boxies*.

   B. Change *boxs* to *boxes*.

   C. Change *boxs* to *boxses*.

   D. Make no change.

> **What is your favorite book about? Write two or three sentences about it.**

_____

_____

_____

Abstract Nouns

A noun can name a person, place, or thing. This kind of noun is a **concrete noun**.

A noun can also name an idea, a feeling, or a quality. This is called an **abstract noun**. You cannot see, hear, taste, smell, or touch an abstract noun.

Suzy got to the finish line first and shouted with <u>joy</u>.

It was <u>luck</u> that Dante arrived right before the bus left.

> **A noun in each sentence is underlined. Write** *abstract* **if the noun names an idea, a feeling, or a quality. Write** *concrete* **if it is a noun you can see, hear, taste, smell, or touch.**

1. Your <u>friendship</u> means a lot to me. _____

2. Jenni took a <u>photograph</u> of a deer in the woods. _____

3. Kyle felt <u>fear</u> as he climbed up to the diving board. _____

4. You have a lot of <u>talent</u> when it comes to painting. _____

5. We found some old clothes of ours in the back of the <u>closet</u>.

   _____

> **Revisit your piece of writing. Edit the draft to make sure all abstract nouns are used correctly.**

Identifying Abstract Nouns

A noun that names an idea, a feeling, or a quality is an **abstract noun**. You cannot see, hear, taste, smell, or touch an abstract noun.

Melissa uses <u>humor</u> to make people feel more comfortable.

I have a wonderful <u>idea</u> for our next play.

▶ **The word in parentheses tells whether the abstract noun in the sentence names an idea, a feeling, or a quality. Write the noun.**

1. It was such a disappointment when we got to the water park and it was

   closed. (feeling). _____

2. Harry didn't have the courage to speak to the famous actor. (quality)

   _____

3. Marissa came up with a plan. (idea) _____

▶ **Write a sentence for each abstract noun.**

4. kindness _____

5. childhood _____

▶ **Revisit your piece of writing. Edit the draft to make sure all abstract nouns are used correctly.**

Abstract Nouns

The subject of a sentence is a noun. It can be concrete or abstract.

A noun that names an idea, a feeling, or a quality is an **abstract noun**.

My <u>brother</u> is known for his <u>bravery</u>.

▶ **Two nouns in each sentence are underlined. Circle the subject of the sentence. Write the abstract noun.**

1. My favorite <u>story</u> is about a <u>friendship</u> between two English girls.

   _____

2. <u>Lola</u> is known for her great <u>memory</u>. _____

3. My <u>mother</u> took me to a march for <u>peace</u>. _____

4. <u>Mr. Jentis</u> read a paragraph and asked for my <u>opinion</u> about it.

   _____

▶ **Choose three abstract nouns from above and write a sentence with them.**

5. _____

6. _____

7. _____

▶ **Revisit your piece of writing. Edit the draft to make sure all abstract nouns are used correctly.**

Review Abstract Nouns

> A noun can name a person, place, or thing. This kind of noun is a **concrete noun**.
>
> A noun can also name an idea, a feeling, or a quality. This is called an **abstract noun**. You cannot see, hear, taste, smell, or touch an abstract noun.

> **▶ Circle the abstract noun in each sentence.**

1. There was confusion in the hallway after the lights suddenly went out.

2. Switzerland is famous for the beauty of its mountains.

3. You will be in big trouble if you drop those glasses.

4. When his brother broke his favorite game, Tom could not control his anger.

5. Mrs. Markle always admired your honesty.

6. I think this science fair project will be a great success.

7. We cannot let this one fight ruin our friendship.

8. I wish you happiness.

9. Halloween is my favorite holiday.

10. I wonder if we will have flying cars in the future.

> **▶ Revisit your piece of writing. Edit the draft to make sure all abstract nouns are used correctly.**

Connect to Writing: Using Abstract Nouns

▶ Read the selection and choose the best answer to each question.

Read the following paragraph about baking a cake. Look for any revisions that should be made. Then answer the questions that follow.

Shanna and her father were baking a carrot cake. (2) It was a delight for them to be baking together. (3) They put all the ingredients into the mixer. (4) The mixer filled with joy. (5) The cake seemed a little flat when it went into the baking pan. (6) Shanna thought something had gone wrong with the mixer. (7) She was worried the whole time the cake was in the oven. (8) But the cake turned out to be a great success!

1. Which of the following sentences uses an abstract noun correctly?

   A. Shanna and her father were baking a carrot cake.

   B. It was a delight for them to be baking together.

   C. They put all the ingredients into the mixer.

   D. The mixer filled with joy.

2. Which of the following sentences uses an abstract noun correctly?

   A. The cake seemed a little flat when it went into the baking pan.

   B. Shanna thought something had gone wrong with the mixer.

   C. She was worried the whole time the cake was in the oven.

   D. But the cake turned out to be a great success!

▶ What is your favorite kind of cake? Write two or three sentences about it.

_____

_____

_____

Changing *y* to *i*

> Add *–s* or *–es* to most singular nouns to form regular plural nouns.
>
> If a noun ends with a consonant and *y*, change the *y* to *i*, and add *–es* to form the plural.
>
> **Singular:**   library   pony
>
> **Plural:**   libraries   ponies

> ▷ **Write the plural form of each singular noun in parentheses. Then write a new sentence using the plural form of the noun.**

1. There is a bush with _____ in our garden. (berry)

   _____

2. I have only visited two large _____ so far. (city)

   _____

3. My mother always says that _____ smell really good. (baby)

   _____

4. We have a jar in our house that is full of _____ . (penny)

   _____

5. What kind of _____ do we need to make this poster? (supply)

   _____

> ▷ **Revisit your piece of writing. Edit the draft to make sure all plural nouns are used correctly.**

Adding –s or –es to Nouns

The spelling of irregular plural nouns changes in a special way.

The <u>woman</u> joined a reading group with other <u>women</u>.

The spelling of some nouns does not change when they are plural.

The black <u>sheep</u> stood out in the field full of white <u>sheep</u>.

The noun *woman* changes to *women* when it is plural.

The noun *sheep* remains *sheep* when it is plural.

> **Write the plural form of each singular noun in parentheses. Then write a new sentence using the plural form of the noun.**

1. Mr. and Mrs. Yoles have three _____ . (child)

_____

2. I grew so fast this year that my shoes no longer fit my _____ ! (foot)

_____

3. There is a family of _____ that live in the tiny hole. (mouse)

_____

4. Charlie has lost both of his front _____ . (tooth)

_____

5. We saw a family of _____ crossing the highway. (deer)

_____

> **Revisit your piece of writing. Edit the draft to make sure all plural nouns are used correctly.**

Forming Irregular Plural Nouns

▶ Write the plural form of each singular noun.

1. pony _____

2. daisy _____

3. candy _____

4. sky _____

5. spy _____

▶ Write *singular* or *plural* for each underlined noun.

6. That basketball player is over seven <u>feet</u> tall. _____

7. The <u>mice</u> came out at night looking for food. _____

8. Look at all the <u>people</u> in the audience! _____

9. Hermione would like to have a <u>child</u> when she grows up. _____

10. A <u>goose</u> chased me around my neighbor's yard. _____

▶ Revisit your piece of writing. Edit the draft to make sure all plural nouns
are used correctly.

Review Plural Nouns

> Form the plural of a noun that ends with a consonant and *y* by changing the *y* to *i* and adding *–es*.
>
> Identify nouns that change their spelling to form their plurals.
>
> The spelling of some nouns does not change to form the plural.
>
> The <u>families</u> sitting on the grass fed the <u>geese</u>.

▶ Write the plural form of the noun in parentheses to complete each sentence.

1. Carrie lost two baby _____ on the same day. (tooth)

2. I love listening to _____ about when my father was little. (story)

3. Can you tell how many _____ are in the room? (person)

4. The two young _____ studied the train schedule. (woman)

5. There were twenty _____ grazing on the hill. (sheep)

6. There are so many _____ around the world that I want to visit. (city)

7. We picked a quart of _____ in one afternoon. (strawberry)

8. There were many _____ today in the garden. (butterfly)

9. These shoes are too tight for my _____ . (foot)

10. The _____ lined up to take turns at the slide. (child)

▶ Revisit your piece of writing. Edit the draft to make sure all plural nouns are used correctly.

Connect to Writing: Using Plural Nouns

▶ **Read the selection and choose the best answer to each question.**

Read the following paragraph about picking fruit at an orchard. Look for any revisions that should be made. Then answer the questions that follow.

(1) Last weekend, we went to an orchard to pick fruit. (2) The orchard had all different kinds of fruit. (3) I think cherrys are my favorite fruit. (4) I also like blueberries, which are easier to pick. (5) When we were done, we had picked five pounds of berries.

1. What change should be made to sentence 3?

   A. Change *cherrys* to *cherreys*.

   B. Change *cherrys* to *cherries*.

   C. Change *favorite* to *favorites*.

   D. Make no change.

2. What change should be made to sentence 5?

   A. Change *berries* to *berrys*.

   B. Change *pounds* to *pound*.

   C. Change *berries* to *berreys*.

   D. Make no change.

▶ **What is your favorite fruit? Write two or three sentences about it.**

_____

_____

_____

Singular Possessive Nouns

A **singular possessive noun** shows that a person, animal, place, or thing has or owns something.

Add an apostrophe and *s* to form a singular possessive noun.

The girl's boots were red.

Andrew's bicycle needs a new tire.

▷ **Write the possessive for each noun below.**

1. lamp _____

2. Jamaica _____

3. detective _____

4. street _____

5. Oliver _____

6. train station _____

▷ **Underline the noun that should be possessive and write the possessive form.**

7. Bobby best friend is Jeremy. _____

8. Her cousin name is Lori. _____

9. My dog favorite food is spaghetti. _____

10. Marie voice is so beautiful. _____

▷ **Revisit a piece of your writing. Edit the draft to make sure all singular possessive nouns are used correctly.**

Plural Possessive Nouns

To form a **plural possessive noun**, add an apostrophe to the end of plural nouns that end in *s*.

Add an apostrophe and *s* to the end of plural nouns that do not end in *s*.

Raymond put the sisters' postcards in the mail.

The children's letters were from all over the country.

> Write the possessive form of the plural nouns.

1. women _____

2. players _____

3. butterflies _____

4. children _____

> Write sentences for three of the possessive plural nouns above.

5. _____

6. _____

7. _____

> Revisit a piece of your writing. Edit the draft to make sure all plural possessive nouns are used correctly.

Possessive Pronouns

Possessive pronouns can take the place of possessive nouns. Possessive pronouns show ownership: *my, your, his, her, its, our, their*.

> **Read the sentences below. Underline the possessive pronouns.**

1. Loraine is our next door neighbor.

2. Is green your favorite color?

3. My mother is one of the funniest people I know.

4. I think that is her notebook.

> **Write a sentence for each of the possessive pronouns.**

5. their _____

6. our _____

7. my _____

> **Revisit a piece of your writing. Edit the draft to make sure all possessive pronouns are used correctly.**

Review Possessive Nouns and Pronouns

> A **possessive noun** shows that a person, place, or thing has or owns something.
>
> Add an apostrophe and *s* to a singular noun to make it possessive. Add an apostrophe to a plural noun that ends in *s*.
>
> **Possessive pronouns** can take the place of possessive nouns. Possessive pronouns show ownership: *my, your, his, her, its, our, their*.
>
> The cat<u>'s</u> water bowl was almost empty.
>
> The boys<u>'</u> sneakers were the same style.
>
> <u>Their</u> favorite breakfast was scrambled eggs and bacon.

▶ **Use the correct possessive form of the noun in parentheses to complete each sentence.**

1. ___Rachel's___ sister is a very fast runner. (Rachel)

2. The ___children's___ section of the library has picture books. (children)

3. The ___clock's___ hands were all broken. (clocks)

▶ **Use a possessive pronoun to take the place of the underlined possessive nouns. Write the pronoun.**

4. The cat jumped onto <u>Jessie's</u> lap. ___her___

5. <u>Monica and Michael's</u> mother is a dentist. _____

▶ **Revisit a piece of your writing. Edit the draft to make sure all possessive nouns and pronouns are used correctly.**

Connect to Writing: Using Possessive Nouns and Pronouns

> **Read the selection and choose the best answer to each question.**

Read the following paragraph about a boy visiting his aunt's farm. Look for any revisions that should be made. Then answer the questions that follow.

(1) Jack's favorite aunt is Jack's Aunt Mona. (2) Jack visits her every summer for two weeks. (3) Jack's Aunt Mona lives on a farm. (4) The farm has vegetables, but there is also a barn full of cows. (5) Jack helps Aunt Mona take care of the cows. (6) The cows' barn is the busiest part of Aunt Mona's farm. (7) But this is what Jack likes the most about visiting Aunt Mona.

1. What change should be made to sentence 1?

    A. Change *Jack's Aunt Mona* to *his Aunt Mona*.

    B. Change *Jack's Aunt Mona* to *Jacks' Aunt Mona*.

    C. Change *Jack's Aunt Mona* to *their Aunt Mona*.

    D. Make no change.

2. What change should be made to sentence 6?

    A. Change *cows' barn* to *cow's barn*.

    B. Change *Aunt Mona's farm* to *Aunt Monas' farm*.

    C. Change *Aunt Mona's farm* to *their farm*.

    D. Make no change.

> **Do you have a favorite relative? Write two or three sentences about him or her.**

_____

_____

_____

Subject Pronouns

A **pronoun** is a word that can take the place of one or more nouns in a sentence. The pronouns *I, you, he, she, it, we,* and *they* are subject pronouns. Pronouns can be singular or plural. A noun and the subject pronoun that replaces it must match each other in singular and plural forms.

The <u>cat</u> jumped on the couch.   <u>It</u> jumped on the couch.

<u>Linda</u> likes chocolate ice cream.   <u>She</u> likes chocolate ice cream.

<u>Our softball team</u> won the game.   <u>We</u> won the game.

> **Write each sentence. Replace the underlined word or words with a subject pronoun.**

1. <u>Benjamin Franklin</u> was a great inventor.

   _____

2. What would <u>Jane</u> like for dinner?

   _____

3. <u>The DeGrassis</u> live next door.

   _____

4. <u>The frog</u> jumped out of the pond.

   _____

5. <u>Larry</u> is almost six feet tall.

   _____

> **Revisit a piece of your writing. Edit the draft to make sure all subject pronouns are used correctly.**

Object Pronouns

The pronouns *me, you, him, her, it, us,* and *them* are called **object pronouns**. Object pronouns follow action verbs and words like *to, for, at, of,* and *with*. A noun and the object pronoun, or antecedent, that replaces it must match each other in singular and plural forms.

The pronouns *it* and *you* are both subject pronouns and object pronouns.

Jessica walked over to <u>Mr. Kelly</u>.   Jessica walked over to <u>him</u>.

A lot of people like <u>gummy bears</u>.   A lot of people like <u>them</u>.

▶ **Write each sentence. Replace the underlined word or words with an object pronoun.**

1. Lily wants to talk to <u>her brother</u>.

_____

2. Did you invite <u>Max and Molly</u> to the party?

_____

3. Harry caught <u>the ball</u>.

_____

4. We really loved <u>the movie</u>.

_____

5. I need to return this book to <u>Anjali</u>.

_____

▶ **Revisit a piece of your writing. Edit the draft to make sure all object pronouns are used correctly.**

Pronoun-Antecedent Agreement

> A **pronoun** can take the place of one or more nouns in a sentence.
>
> An **antecedent** is the noun or noun phrase to which a pronoun refers. An antecedent usually comes before the pronoun, but it may come after. Pronouns and antecedents must agree in number, person, and gender.
>
> I liked <u>my</u> story.
>
> Allie liked <u>her</u> story.
>
> Jeff and Maggie liked <u>their</u> story.

▶ **Complete each sentence by writing the pronoun that agrees with the underlined antecedent. Remember to make sure the pronoun and antecedent match in number, person, and gender.**

1. <u>Alicia and Andrew</u> made a cake for _____ mother.

2. <u>I</u> said, "Let _____ see that!"

3. After _____ finished his project, <u>David</u> went home.

4. <u>Natalie</u> loves to take _____ dog over to the dog park.

5. <u>We</u> were so proud of _____ team when we won the game.

▶ **Revisit a piece of your writing. Edit the draft to make sure all pronoun-antecedent agreement is used correctly.**

Review Pronouns

A **pronoun** is a word that can take the place of one or more nouns in a sentence. The pronouns *I, you, he, she, it, we,* and *they* are subject pronouns.

The pronouns *me, you, him, her, it, us,* and *them* are called **object pronouns**. Object pronouns follow action verbs and words like *to, for, at, of,* and *with*. A noun and the object pronoun, or antecedent, that replaces it must match each other in singular and plural forms.

▶ **Write each sentence. Replace the underlined word or words with a pronoun.**

1. <u>Rabbits</u> love to eat spinach.

   _____

2. I hope you didn't forget <u>my sister, Marcia</u>.

   _____

3. We need to collect <u>leaves</u> for a collage.

   _____

4. Have you ever met <u>Albert and Tina</u>?

   _____

5. <u>Ricky</u> has been my friend since kindergarten.

   _____

▶ **Revisit a piece of your writing. Edit the draft to make sure all pronouns are used correctly.**

Connect to Writing: Using Pronouns

▶ **Read the selection and choose the best answer to each question.**

Read the following paragraph about writing a story. Look for any revisions that should be made. Then answer the questions that follow.

(1) Jessie and I worked on a story together. (2) We spent one week writing the story. (3) Then we showed it to our teacher. (4) Our teacher thought the story was good. (5) But she told we that the story needed an ending. (6) The story was about two kids writing a story. (7) The kids show their story to their teacher. (8) We thought that was the ending!

1. What change should be made to sentence 3?

   A. Change *we* to *us*.

   B. Change *it* to *them*.

   C. Change *it* to *her*.

   D. Make no change.

2. What change should be made to sentence 5?

   A. Change *we* to *us*.

   B. Change *we* to *she*.

   C. Change *she* to *her*.

   D. Make no change.

▶ **What would you write a story about? Write two or three sentences about it.**

_____

_____

_____

Using *I* and *Me*

Use the pronoun *I* only as the subject of a sentence. Always capitalize the word *I*.

> I have two sisters.

Use the pronoun *me* only as an object pronoun. When you talk about another person and yourself, it is polite to list yourself last.

> Henry is friends with Julie and me.

▶ **Write the pronoun *I* or *me* to complete each sentence.**

1. _____I_____ ran in the 50-yard dash.

2. Kenneth and _____I_____ made cupcakes for the party.

3. Please return that movie to _____me_____ .

4. This morning _____I_____ saw a bluebird in the backyard.

5. The dog ran over to Laura and _____me_____ .

6. My mother took Debbie and _____me_____ to the mall.

7. Will you please give _____me_____ a piece of gum?

8. My brother and _____I_____ look alike.

9. Marshall and _____I_____ play on the same team.

10. My grandmother knitted a hat for _____me_____ .

▶ **Revisit a piece of your writing. Edit the draft to make sure the pronouns *I* and *me* are used correctly.**

Pronouns and Homophones

Homophones are words that sound alike but have different spellings and different meanings. Be sure to choose the correct homophone. Using the wrong homophone changes the meaning of the sentence.

Homophone	Meaning	Example
its	belonging to it	The cat licked its paw.
it's	it is	It's going to be hot today.
your	belonging to you	I like your glasses.
you're	you are	You're a good friend.
there	at or in that place	Please put the plates there.
their	belonging to them	That is their red car.
they're	they are	They're coming over later.

▶ **Read the sentences. Circle the correct homophones.**

1. This fish is too big for (its, it's) tank.

2. Is (there, their) a good restaurant in town?

3. Did you see anything interesting on (your, you're) walk?

4. I bet (they're, there) looking forward to meeting you.

5. (Your, You're) the best ice skater I know!

▶ **Revisit a piece of your writing. Edit the draft to make sure all pronouns and homophones are used correctly.**

Using Pronouns *I, Me, Its, Their, Your*

> Use the pronoun *I* only as the subject of a sentence.
>
> Use the pronoun *me* only as an object pronoun.

▶ **Read each pair of sentences. Circle the letter next to the sentence that uses the correct pronoun.**

1. **A.** Dad and I will be walking the dog tonight.
   B. Dad and me will be walking the dog tonight.

2. **A.** Justin invited Alison and I to the movies.
   B. Justin invited Alison and me to the movies.

3. **A.** Coco and me are best friends.
   B. Coco and I are best friends.

4. **A.** Will Kevin and I be in the same class next year?
   B. Will Kevin and me be in the same class next year?

5. **A.** Do you want to go on a walk with my sister and I?
   B. Do you want to go on a walk with my sister and me?

▶ **Revisit a piece of your writing. Edit the draft to make sure all pronouns are used correctly.**

Review Correct Pronouns

Use the pronoun *I* only as the subject of a sentence. Always capitalize the word *I*.

Use the pronoun *me* only as an object pronoun. When you talk about another person and yourself, it is polite to list yourself last.

Homophones are words that sound alike but have different spellings and different meanings. Be sure to choose the correct homophone.

Homophone	Meaning
its	belonging to it
it's	it is
your	belonging to you
you're	you are
there	at or in that place
their	belonging to them
they're	they are

> **Read the sentences. Circle the correct word in parentheses.**

1. I told the Gelmans that (they're, their) my favorite neighbors.

2. Can Debbie and (me, I) take your dog for a walk?

3. We do not think (its, it's) going to rain today.

4. I hope (you're, your) really sure about this.

5. Lots of people piled (their, they're) coats on the bleachers.

> **Revisit a piece of your writing. Edit the draft to make sure all pronouns are used correctly.**

Connect to Writing: Proofreading

> Read the selection and choose the best answer to each question.

Read the following paragraph about a new friend. Look for any revisions that should be made. Then answer the questions that follow.

(1) A new girl came to our class today. (2) Her name is Jackie. (3) Jackie sat with Min Jin and I during lunch. (4) We found out that Jackie lives not too far from either of us. (5) We had a really good time talking at lunch. (6) There both coming to my house after school today.

1. What change should be made to sentence 3?

 A. *Min Jin and I* should be *me and Min Jin.*
 B. *Min Jin and I* should be *I and Min Jin.*
 C. *Min Jin and I* should be *Min Jin and me.*
 D. Make no change.

2. What change should be made to sentence 6?

 A. *There* should be *They're.*
 B. *There* should be *Their.*
 C. *There* should be *Theyr.*
 D. Make no change.

> What is something you would like to do with some friends after school? Write two or three sentences about it.

_____

_____

_____

Action Verbs

Words that show action, or something that is done,
are **action verbs**.

The dog <u>ran</u> across the yard.

The cat <u>looked</u> out the window.

> **Each sentence has one action verb. Write the action verb on the line.**

1. We ate dinner last night at seven. _____

2. The child slept in the nap room. _____

3. Janet played soccer with her teammates. _____

4. Please open the door for me. _____

5. What should we bring to the party? _____

6. The baby smiled at me. _____

7. Kaylie and I sing in the choir. _____

8. I helped my mother with the groceries. _____

9. Anthony threw the football to me. _____

10. The cat licked its paw. _____

> **Revisit a piece of your writing. Edit the draft to make sure all action verbs are used correctly.**

Being Verbs

Some verbs do not show action. The verbs *am, is, are, was,* and *were* are forms of the verb *be.* They tell what someone or something is or was. *Am, is,* and *are* show present tense. *Was* and *were* show past tense.

> I am happy to be here.
> They are good friends.
> You were the first person I met.

> **Write the *being* verb on the line. Write present or past for each verb.**

1. Danny was nice to his brother. _____ was

2. She is ten years old. _____ is

3. I was swimming in the pool. _____ was

4. We were just going to call you. _____ were

5. You are older than me by one day. _____ are

6. Lilia was late for her appointment. _____ was

7. I am cooking dinner tonight. _____ am

8. We were waiting in line for our tickets. _____ were

9. Jenny and I are playing a game. _____ are

10. I am happy about our trip. _____ am

> **Revisit a piece of your writing. Edit the draft to make sure all *being* verbs are used correctly.**

Action Verbs and *Being* Verbs

▶ **There is one action verb in each sentence. Write the verb on the line.**

1. I looked for my gloves. _____

2. Daria opened the box carefully. _____

3. The cat jumped onto the couch. _____

4. We laughed at Katie's joke. _____

5. The teacher read a story. _____

▶ **Write the *being* verb on the line. Then write *present* or *past*.**

6. I am interested in dinosaurs. _____

7. You were happy to visit me. _____

8. Josh was excited to play. _____

9. The sun is bright today. _____

10. They are my mother's sisters. _____

▶ **Revisit a piece of your writing. Edit the draft to make sure all action verbs
and *being* verbs are used correctly.**

Reviewing Action and *Being* Verbs

> Words that show action, or something that is done, are action verbs.
>
> The verbs *am, is, are, was,* and *were* are forms of the verb *be.* They tell what someone or something is or was.

> **There is one action verb in each sentence. Write the verb on the line.**

1. Ramona caught the ball. _____

2. Howie found a penny. _____

3. My father and I baked brownies. _____

4. The elephant lifted its trunk. _____

5. We bought desserts for the party. _____

> **Write the *being* verb on the line.**

6. We were surprised when it snowed. _____

7. You are younger than my brother. _____

8. I am worried about swim class. _____

9. Debbie is going to Texas. _____

10. Nick and Div were late for class. _____.

> **Revisit a piece of your writing. Edit the draft to make sure all action verbs and *being* verbs are used correctly.**

Connect to Writing: Using Action and *Being* Verbs

▶ **Read the selection and choose the best answer to each question.**

Read the following paragraph about a pet bearded dragon. Look for any revisions that should be made. Then answer the questions that follow.

(1) My brother has a bearded dragon. (2) The name of the dragon are Mango. (3) Mango sleeps on a big branch in his cage. (4) He wakes up when he is hungry. (5) Mango eat lots of vegetables. (6) He loves spinach most of all. (7) Mango is really silly sometimes. (8) Bearded dragons are great pets.

1. What statement is not written correctly?

   A. My brother has a bearded dragon.

   B. The name of the dragon are Mango.

   C. Mango sleeps on a big branch in his cage.

   D. He wakes up when he is hungry.

2. What statement correctly uses an action verb?

   A. Mango eat lots of vegetables.

   B. He loves spinach most of all.

   C. Mango is really silly sometimes.

   D. Bearded dragons are great pets.

▶ **Do you think you would like a bearded dragon for a pet? Write two or three sentences about it.**

_____

_____

_____

_____

Present and Past Tense

Many verbs in the present tense have an *−s* ending with a singular subject. Verbs in the present tense do not have an *−s* ending with a plural subject. Most verbs in the past tense have an *−ed* ending.

A boy <u>opens</u> the box.	present
Two boys <u>open</u> the box.	present
A boy <u>opened</u> the box.	past

▶ **Write** *present* **if the underlined verb shows the present tense. Write** *past* **if the underlined verb shows the past tense.**

1. We <u>need</u> some cinnamon for this French toast. _____

2. I <u>remember</u> you from first grade. _____

3. Justine and I <u>walk</u> home together. _____

4. I <u>played</u> a wolf in the school musical. _____

5. They <u>offered</u> to watch our dog. _____

6. Nick <u>laughs</u> when I tell jokes. _____

7. We <u>kicked</u> the ball to the goal line. _____

8. Jackson <u>waits</u> for me at the bus stop. _____

9. Kristen <u>packed</u> her suitcase for the trip. _____

10. The mouse <u>squealed</u> and ran away. _____

▶ **Revisit a piece of your writing. Edit the draft to make sure all verb tenses are used correctly.**

Present, Past, and Future Tense

Many verbs in the present tense with singular subjects use an –s ending.
Verbs in the present tense with plural subjects do not use an –s ending.

Many verbs in the past tense use an –ed ending.

Verbs in the future tense use the helping verb will.

The girl <u>dances</u> on the stage.	present
The girls <u>dance</u> on the stage.	present
The girl <u>danced</u> on the stage.	past
The girl <u>will dance</u> on the stage.	future

▶ **Write present if the underlined verb shows present tense. Write past if the underlined verb shows past tense. Write future if the underlined verb shows future tense.**

1. The dog <u>chewed</u> on a bone. _____

2. I <u>will explain</u> how this game works. _____

3. Teddy and Lailia <u>peel</u> carrots for the salad. _____

4. I <u>looked</u> for you in the park. _____

5. The moon <u>will shine</u> in the sky tonight. _____

▶ **Revisit a piece of your writing. Edit the draft to make sure all verb tenses are used correctly.**

Present, Past, and Future Tense

A verb that explains an action that has already happened shows past tense.

A verb that tells about an action happening now shows present tense.

A verb that tells about an action that will happen in the future shows future tense.

> Write *present* if the underlined verb shows present tense. Write *past* if the underlined verb shows past tense. Write *future* if the underlined verb shows future tense.

1. My mother and I <u>walked</u> in the woods. _____

2. Kyle <u>shouted</u> something, but I did not hear what he said. _____

3. We <u>will see</u> a movie this weekend. _____

4. We <u>picked</u> raspberries in my grandmother's backyard. _____

5. Julia <u>ordered</u> some new books. _____

6. My father <u>votes</u> in the election. _____

7. Denise <u>will visit</u> us in the summer. _____

8. Mr. Jacobs <u>coached</u> our softball team. _____

9. I <u>will drink</u> two glasses of water. _____

10. We <u>listen</u> to the sounds outside our window. _____

> Revisit a piece of your writing. Edit the draft to make sure all verb tenses are used correctly.

Review Verb Tenses

> Verbs in the present tense tell that the action in the sentence is happening now. Use an *–s* ending for singular subjects and no *–s* ending for a plural subject.
>
> Verbs in the past tense tell about action in the sentence that has already happened. Many verbs add *–ed* to show past tense.
>
> Verbs that tell about an action that is going to happen are in the future tense. You use the helping verb *will*.
>
> I <u>cook</u> pancakes. Yesterday I <u>cooked</u> blueberry pancakes. I <u>will cook</u> banana pancakes tomorrow.

▶ **Write *present, past,* or *future* for the tense each verb shows.**

1. We <u>will rake</u> leaves for our neighbor. _____

2. Jonas <u>jumps</u> over the rain puddle. _____

3. Monica and I <u>danced</u> in the ballet recital. _____

▶ **Rewrite sentences with underlined verbs from this paragraph. Change each underlined verb to make it match the tense of the verb in the first sentence. Write the new sentences on the lines below.**

My sister cooked dinner last night. She <u>works</u> on dinner for two hours. Then she <u>will call</u> us to the dinner table.

4. _____

5. _____

▶ **Revisit a piece of your writing. Edit the draft to make sure all verb tenses are used correctly.**

Connect to Writing: Using Present, Past, and Future Tense

> **Read the selection and choose the best answer to each question.**
Read the following paragraph about watching a movie. Look for any revisions that should be made. Then answer the questions that follow.

(1) Last night, we watched a new movie. (2) My sister wanted to watch a scary movie. (3) I did not. (4) I will remember that I had bad dreams last time. (5) So I offered to find a funny movie. (6) It seems very good to me. (7) I was right! (8) We laughed all night long.

1. Which statement has a verb that is written in the wrong tense?

   A. Last night, we watched a new movie.

   B. My sister wanted to watch a scary movie.

   C. I did not.

   D. I will remember that I had bad dreams last time.

2. What change should be made to sentence 6?

   A. It should be written in the past tense.

   B. It should be written in the present tense.

   C. It should be written in the future tense.

   D. Make no change.

> **What kind of movie do you like to watch? Write two or three sentences about it.**

_____

_____

_____

Verbs in the Past

Most verbs show past tense by adding –ed.

Some verbs end with e. Drop the e and add –ed.

> They skipped across the playground. (skipped is
> the past-tense verb)

> He wanted to add chocolate to the cake recipe.
> (wanted is the past-tense verb)

> Sam's parents loved his science presentation.
> (loved is the past-tense verb)

▶ **Write each sentence using the correct past tense of the verb in parentheses.**

1. Sarah _____ to get Martha a birthday present. (want)

2. Ms. Jones _____ on Jim during the math lesson. (call)

3. Many third grade students _____ kickball. (play)

4. Jim and I _____ our science presentation. (practice)

5. We _____ to eat at home instead of going to a restaurant.
   (decide)

▶ **Revisit a piece of your writing. Edit the draft to make sure all verbs in the past tense are used correctly.**

_____

_____

Verbs in the Present

Add –s to most present-tense verbs when the noun in the subject is singular. For most verbs that end in y, change the y to i and add –es.

Do not add –s to the verb when the noun in the subject is plural.

Do not add –s to the verb when the subject is I or you.

Josh <u>sits</u> in the dining room. He <u>reads</u> to his sister. (*sits* and *reads* are present-tense verbs)

We <u>sit</u> together. We <u>read</u> together. (*sit* and *read* are present-tense verbs)

I <u>sit</u> alone. I <u>read</u> with my sister. (*sit* and *read* are present-tense verbs)

▶ **Write each sentence using the correct present tense of the verb in parentheses.**

1. Bert _____ to pick up Aaron at the airport. (drive)

2. Aaron's flight _____ at 9:30. (arrive)

3. I _____ to go to the airport. (want)

4. The airplane _____ to be refueled. (need)

5. The mechanics _____ the plane to make sure it is ready for the next flight. (check)

▶ **Revisit a piece of your writing. Edit the draft to make sure all verbs in the present tense are used correctly.**

Verbs in the Future

A verb that tells about an action that will happen is in the future tense.

Add the word *will* before a verb to form the future tense.

I <u>will go</u> to the carnival. (adding *will* before *go* forms the future tense)

My family <u>will ride</u> the roller coaster. (adding *will* before *ride* forms the future tense)

▷ Write each sentence using the correct future tense of the verb in parentheses.

1. Steve _____ John to go to the carnival with his family. (invite)

2. I _____ my parents if we can go, too. (ask)

3. Our families _____ the ferris wheel together. (ride)

4. I _____ pink cotton candy. (buy)

5. We _____ after dark. (leave)

▷ Revisit a piece of your writing. Edit the draft to make sure all verbs in the future tense are used correctly.

Name _____

Review Verb Tenses

> Verbs in the present tense tell that the action in the sentence is happening now. Use an *–s* ending for singular subjects and no ending for a plural subject.
>
> Verbs in the past tense tell about action in the sentence that has already happened. Many verbs add *–ed* to show past tense.
>
> Verbs that tell about an action that is going to happen are in the future tense. You use the helping verb *will*.
>
> I <u>work</u> today. Yesterday I <u>worked</u>. I <u>will work</u> tomorrow. (*work* is the present tense; *worked* is the past tense, *will work* is the future tense)

▶ **Circle the verb in each sentence. Write the tense of the verb on the line.**

1. Last summer we camped by the lake. _____

2. We will go to the same campground this summer. _____

3. I roll up my sleeping bag. _____

▶ **Rewrite sentences with underlined verbs in this paragraph. Change each underlined verb to make it match the tense of the verb in the first sentence. Write new sentences on the lines below.**

> The weather was sunny and warm. We <u>go</u> fishing every day. I <u>will sleep</u> well under the stars.

4. _____

5. _____

▶ **Revisit a piece of your writing. Edit the draft to make sure all verbs in the future tense are used correctly.**

Grade 3 • Verb Tenses II

Connect to Writing: Using Past, Present, and Future Tenses

▶ **Read the selection and choose the best answer to each question.**

Ahmed wrote the following paragraph about his family's summer vacation. Read his paragraph and look for revisions he should make. Then answer the questions that follow.

(1) During the summer we drive to the beach. (2) Last summer we camp in the mountains. (3) Last summer I also hike up a steep trail. (4) Next summer we roast marshmallows over the campfire. (5) I love camping.

1. Which statement contains a verb in the proper tense?

   A. Last summer we camp in the mountains.

   B. Last summer I also hike up a steep trail.

   C. Next summer we roast marshmallows over the campfire.

   D. I love camping.

2. Which statement below is a properly edited verison of statement 3?

   A. Last summer I also hike up a steep trail.

   B. Last summer I also hiking up a steep trail.

   C. Last summer I am also hiking up a steep trail.

   D. Last summer I also hiked up a steep trail.

▶ **What kind of outdoor activities do you enjoy? Write two or three sentences about it.**

_____

_____

_____

The Verb *Be*

> The verb *be* has different forms. Different subjects use these different forms. *Am, are,* and *is* show present tense. *Was* and *were* show past tense.
>
> Modern Art <u>was</u> the focus of our art unit last month. (*was* is the past tense)
>
> We <u>were</u> interested in the artwork. (*were* is the past tense)
>
> One famous modern artist <u>is</u> Jasper Johns. (*is* is the present tense)

▶ Choose the correct verb in parentheses, and write it on the line.

1. My art project (am, is) not done yet. _____

2. Mr. Jones (was, were) teaching us about modern artists. _____

3. Abstract figures (was, were) part of my painting. _____

4. They (was, were) very interesting shapes. _____

5. Melissa's project (is, are) about nature. _____

6. Trees and moss (is, are) in her drawing. _____

7. She (is, are) interested in nature. _____

8. We (am, are) working hard to finish our projects. _____

9. The projects (is, are) hanging on the wall. _____

10. Our room (is, are) an art gallery! _____

▶ Revisit a piece of your writing. Edit the draft to make sure all verbs are used correctly.

Helping Verbs

Helping verbs work with the main verb to help show time.

Subject	Helping Verbs
Singular nouns Pronouns: he, she, it	is, was, has
Plural nouns Pronouns: you, we, they	are, have, were
Pronoun: I	am, was, have

The snow <u>was</u> getting deeper.   It <u>was</u> freezing cold outside.

The friends <u>were</u> sledding together.   They <u>were</u> dressed warmly.

It <u>was</u> blustery.   The snowstorm <u>has</u> stopped.

I <u>was</u> excited about the summer.

▶ **Write the correct verb in parentheses to complete the sentence.**

1. The workers (is, are) building a new skyscraper. _____

2. I (has, have) asked him to show me the construction site. _____

3. I (am, is) going to wear a hard hat for safety. _____

4. They (has, have) dug an enormous hole in the ground. _____

5. Many trucks (was, were) driving around the construction site. _____

▶ **Revisit a piece of your writing. Edit the draft to make sure all verbs are used correctly.**

Using the Verbs *Be* and *Have*

Helping verbs work with the main verb to help show time.

Singular and plural subjects use different forms.

Subject	Helping Verbs
Singular nouns Pronouns: he, she, it	is, was, has
Plural nouns Pronouns: you, we, they	are, have, were
Pronoun: I	am, was, have

She <u>has</u> worked in the library.

I <u>am</u> having a sandwich for lunch.

▶ **Choose the correct verb in parentheses, and write it on the line.**

1. She (is, are) going to the museum. _____

2. I (has, have) visited many times. _____

3. We (is, are) studying Ancient Egypt in our class. _____

4. Our teacher (has, have) shown us pictures of pyramids. _____

5. We (has, have) learned many interesting facts. _____

▶ **Revisit a piece of your writing. Edit the draft to make sure all verbs are used correctly.**

Review the Verb *Be* and Helping Verbs

The verb *be* has different forms. Different subjects use these different forms. *Am, is,* and *are* show present tense. *Was* and *were* show past tense.

Helping verbs work with the main verb to help show time.

Singular and plural subjects use different forms.

Sarah <u>will be</u> the next class president.

I <u>am</u> going to vote for her.

The rest of the class <u>has</u> already voted.

I <u>have</u> told everyone that Sarah <u>will</u> do a good job.

▷ **Choose the correct verb in parentheses, and write it on the line.**

1. The zoo (is, are) crowded today. _____ is

2. I (has, have) been wanting to go there. _____ have

3. I (has, have) heard that there are baby pandas there. _____ have

4. James (am, is) going to the zoo tomorrow. _____ is

5. He (has, have) been there many times. _____ has

▷ **Revisit a piece of your writing. Edit the draft to make sure all verbs with *be* and helping verbs are used correctly.**

Connect to Writing: Using the Verb *Be* and Helping Verbs

> **Read the selection and choose the best answer to each question.**

Jack wrote the following paragraph about favorite things to do. Read his paragraph and look for revisions he should make. Then answer the questions that follow.

(1) Jack loves to swim. (2) His sister loves to swim. (3) Jack has been on the swim team. (4) He is going to be a lifeguard. (5) Jack swims in the summer. (6) Jack swims in the winter.

1. Which statement best combines statements 1 and 2?

   A. Jack loves to swim and his sister loves to swim, too.

   B. Jack and his sister love to swim.

   C. Jack loves swimming and Jack's sister loves swimming.

   D. Jack loves swimming and so does his sister.

2. Which statement uses a helping verb to describe something that will happen in the future?

   A. Jack loves to swim.

   B. Jack has been on the swim team.

   C. He is going to be a lifeguard.

   D. Jack swims in the summer.

> **Do you enjoy swimming? Have you ever swam in the ocean? Write two or three sentences about it.**

_____

_____

_____

Come, Do, Go, Run, See

The verbs *come, do, go, run,* and *see* are irregular and have special spellings to show past tense.

These verbs may also have other spellings when they are used with *has, had,* or *have.*

> A gazelle had <u>run</u> across the field.

> The gazelle <u>ran</u> across the field yesterday.

▶ **Write the correct past tense of the verb in parentheses to complete each sentence.**

1. Davia had (come, came) home with Danielle after school. _____

2. Rashawn (saw, seen) his friend at the park. _____

3. The cat has (ran, run) away from home before. _____

4. Ben (did, done) some math homework while I read. _____

5. Sarah (went, gone) home after dinner. _____

▶ **Revisit a piece of your writing. Edit the draft to make sure all irregular verbs are used correctly.**

Eat, Give, Grow, Take, Write

The verbs *eat*, *give*, *grow*, *take*, and *write* have special spellings to show past tense. These verbs also have other spellings when they are used with *has, had,* or *have.*

My teacher <u>gave</u> me a sharpened pencil to use.

That author has <u>written</u> many books I love.

▶ **Write the correct past tense of the verb in parentheses to complete each sentence.**

1. I (wrote, written) my autobiography. _____

2. We had (eaten, ate) supper before we went to the game. _____

3. Mrs. Sanchez gave me some tomatoes she (grown, grew) in her garden.

   _____

4. Marissa had (took, taken) piano lessons before she moved here.

   _____

5. Bart (gave, give) his dog a treat. _____

▶ **Revisit a piece of your writing. Edit the draft to make sure all irregular verbs are used correctly.**

Using Irregular Verbs

The verbs *come, do, go, run, see, eat, give, grow, take,* and *write* are irregular and have special spellings to show past tense.

These verbs may also have other spellings when they are used with *has, had,* or *have.*

> Jack <u>ran</u> down the sidewalk to meet the mail carrier.
>
> The tomato plants <u>grew</u> tall last summer.
>
> I <u>have done</u> all I can to prepare for the test.

▷ **Write the correct past tense of the verb in parentheses to complete each sentence.**

1. I have (took, taken) many pictures of trees. _____

2. The tree in my yard has (grew, grown) very tall. _____

3. We (ate, eaten) lunch under the big oak tree last week. _____

4. I (wrote, written) a story about the maple tree in my yard. _____

5. My parents (gave, given) me a tiny tree to plant outside my window. _____

▷ **Revisit a piece of your writing. Edit the draft to make sure all irregular verbs are used correctly.**

Review Irregular Verbs

The verbs *come, do, go, run, see, eat, give, grow, take,* and *write* are irregular and have special spellings to show past tense.

These verbs may also have other spellings when they are used with *has, had,* or *have.*

Ron <u>did</u> his homework last night.

He <u>had gone</u> to the football game the night before.

I <u>ate</u> dinner at Sam's house yesterday.

> **Use the proper past-tense form of the verb in parentheses.**

1. The plants in the sun _____ taller than the ones in the shade. (grow)

2. We _____ a famous garden in Paris, France. (see)

3. They _____ a picnic lunch at a table in the garden. (eat)

4. I _____ a poem about the roses in the garden. (write)

5. My parents _____ a photo of me next to an enormous sunflower. (take)

> **Revisit a piece of your writing. Edit the draft to make sure all irregular verbs are used correctly.**

Connect to Writing: Using Irregular Verbs

▶ **Read the selection and choose the best answer to each question.**

Laura wrote the following paragraph about her science fair project. Read her paragraph and look for revisions she should make. Then answer the questions that follow.

(1) I seen an interesting display at my local science museum about volcanoes. (2) I go there with my class for a field trip last week. (3) I got the idea to do my science fair project about volcanoes. (4) That night, after I eaten dinner, I started working on it. (5) I gave it my best effort, but I couldn't make the volcano erupt!

1. Which statement uses a proper version of an irregular verb?

   A. I seen an interesting display at my local science museum about volcanoes.

   B. I go there with my class for a field trip last week.

   C. That night, after I eaten dinner, I started working on it.

   D. I gave it my best effort, but I couldn't make the volcano erupt!

2. Which statement below is a properly edited verison of statement 2?

   A. I go there with my class for a field trip last week.

   B. I went there with my class for a field trip last week.

   C. I going there with my class for a field trip last week.

   D. I gone there with my class for a field trip last week.

▶ **What types of science experiments have you done? Write two or three sentences about it.**

_____

_____

_____

Adjectives That Tell What Kind

> **Adjectives** describe nouns. Some adjectives tell what kind. Choose adjectives carefully.
>
> Tanner wore a <u>striped</u> shirt.
>
> Blair's aunt drives a <u>pink</u> pickup truck.

▶ **Write the adjective that tells about the underlined noun.**

1. Our class worked on a reading <u>project</u>. _____

2. Mr. Jones put several interesting <u>books</u> on the table. _____

3. The longest <u>book</u> was chosen last. _____

4. Jack chose the novel with the colorful <u>cover</u>. _____

5. Lisa chose a paperback <u>book</u> about Harriet Tubman _____

6. Mary created a big <u>poster</u> for her report. _____

7. Yaz explained the complicated <u>plot</u> of her book. _____

8. We visited the large <u>library</u> afterwards. _____

9. The librarian helped us pick similar <u>books</u> to read. _____

10. Jadon found his book in the biography <u>section</u> of the library.

    _____

▶ **Revisit a piece of your writing. Edit the draft to make sure all adjectives are used correctly.**

Adjectives That Tell How Many

An **adjective** is a word that describes, or tells about, a noun. Some adjectives tell how many. An adjective that tells how many comes before the noun it describes.

She saw <u>three</u> birds in a nest. (How many birds are in the nest?)

There are <u>several</u> dogs in the park. (How many dogs were in the park?)

> Write the adjective that tells how many about the underlined noun.

1. I have ten <u>fingers</u>. _____

2. The tomato plant has twelve <u>tomatoes</u>. _____

3. There are several <u>people</u> interested in the show. _____

4. The garbage will fit in two <u>bags</u>. _____

5. The book was loved by many <u>children</u>. _____

6. Sarah has three <u>cats</u>. _____

7. Kate needs ten <u>buttons</u> for the sweater she is knitting. _____

8. The book has 600 <u>pages</u>. _____

9. There are five <u>kinds</u> of burgers on the menu. _____

10. The island is one <u>mile</u> away. _____

> Revisit a piece of your writing. Edit the draft to make sure all adjectives are used correctly.

This, That, and Articles

The adjectives *this* and *that* tell "which one."

The words *a, an,* and *the* are adjectives called **articles**.

Use *a* before nouns that begin with a consonant sound.
Use *an* before nouns that begin with a vowel sound.

▶ **Underline the adjective that tells which one. Write the noun the adjective describes.**

1. Please bring me that newspaper. _____

2. This bridge is being repaired. _____

3. There's an interesting story about that boy. _____

4. This room is a mess. _____

▶ **Circle the article in parentheses to go with the underlined word.**

5. I have (a, an) <u>bicycle</u>.

6. Please add air to (the, an) <u>tires</u>.

7. Have you ever flown in (a, an) <u>airplane</u>?

8. I keep my skateboard in (the, an) <u>garage</u>.

9. I'll bring (a, an) <u>apple</u> for a snack.

10. I cut out (a, an) <u>article</u> from a newspaper.

▶ **Revisit a piece of your writing. Edit the draft to make sure all adjectives are used correctly.**

Review Adjectives and Articles

> The words *a, an,* and *the* are special adjectives called **articles**. Use *a* and *an* with singular nouns. Use *a* before words that begin with a consonant sound. Use *an* before words that begin with a vowel sound. Use *the* before both singular and plural nouns.
>
> Adjectives that tell what kind or how much usually come before the noun they describe.

▶ **Rewrite each sentence, adding an adjective to describe the underlined noun.**

1. We saw <u>mountains</u> at Yosemite National Park.

   _____

2. There were also hiking <u>trails</u> around the park.

   _____

▶ **Correct the paragraph below, using *a, an,* and *the* correctly.**

   We took an road trip to see Yellowstone National Park. It is a most popular national park in the United States. We saw the tall mountain and an geyser.

   _____

   _____

   _____

▶ **Revisit a piece of your writing. Edit the draft to make sure all adjectives are used correctly.**

Connect to Writing: Using Adjectives and Articles

> **Read the selection and choose the best answer to each question.**

Julissa wrote the following paragraph about her hospital visit. Read her paragraph and look for revisions she should make. Then answer the questions that follow.

(1) We went to the hospital. (2) The hospital is new. (3) There are doctors in the new hospital. (4) There are many doctors. (5) There are many examination rooms. (6) The examination rooms are clean. (7) The kind doctor came to see me. (8) She gave me a bandage for my cut. (9) The bandage was soft.

1. Which statement below is the best combination of statements 1 and 2?

   A. We went to a hospital that was a new hospital.

   B. We went to a new hospital.

   C. We went somewhere new it was a hospital.

   D. We went to a hospital, it was new.

2. Which statement combines two shorter ideas into one statement?

   A. There are many doctors.

   B. There are many examination rooms.

   C. She gave me a soft bandage for my cut.

   D. The bandage was soft.

> **Have you ever been to the the doctor's office? Write two or three sentences about it using adjectives to describe your experience.**

_____

_____

_____

Adding *–er, –ier,* and *More*

Add *–er* to most adjectives that have one syllable.

For adjectives that have two syllables and end in *–y,* such as *happy,* replace the *y* with *i* and then add *–er.*

Add *more* before adjectives that have two or more syllables.

> The basketball is <u>larger</u> than a baseball.
>
> The new baseball was <u>cleaner</u> than the used baseball.
>
> The baseball stadium is <u>noisier</u> than the basketball arena.
>
> I think basketball is <u>more difficult</u> than baseball.

▶ **Circle the correct form of the adjective in parentheses.**

1. The (younger, more young) of my two sisters wanted to go to the grocery store with Mom.

2. The watermelon is (larger, more large) than the cantaloupe.

3. The cantaloupe is (more sweet, sweeter) than the watermelon.

4. Lasagna is (difficulter, more difficult) to make than soup.

5. The grocery store is (interestinger, more interesting) than the auto repair shop.

▶ **Revisit a piece of your writing. Edit the draft to make sure all adjectives are used correctly.**

Name _____

One-Syllable Adjectives That Compare

Add *–er* to most adjectives that have one syllable.

For adjectives with one syllable that end in a single vowel followed by a consonant, double the last consonant and then add *–er*.

Is the weather <u>colder</u> in Minnesota?

▷ **Write the correct form of the adjective on the line.**

1. big _____

2. mad _____

3. fair _____

4. red _____

5. soft _____

6. high _____

7. long _____

8. wise _____

9. quick _____

10. fat _____

▷ **Revisit a piece of your writing. Edit the draft to make sure all adjectives are used correctly.**

Compare More Than Two Nouns

Add *-est* to most adjectives that have one syllable.

For adjectives with two or more syllables, add the word *most* before the adjective.

For adjectives with two syllables that end in *-y*, such as *happy*, replace the *y* with an *i* and then add *-est*.

For adjectives that have one syllable and end in a single vowel followed by a consonant, first double the last consonant and then add *-est*.

Which of the state's parks are the <u>largest</u>?

She ordered the <u>most expensive</u> meal.

Of the three burgers, Jack's is the <u>tastiest</u>.

▶ **Write the correct form of the adjective that compares more than two nouns.**

1. hot _____

2. interesting _____

3. delicious _____

4. fast _____

5. low _____

▶ **Revisit a piece of your writing. Edit the draft to make sure all adjectives are used correctly.**

Review Adjectives That Compare

Adjectives are used to describe how people, places, or things are alike or different. Some adjectives use different endings to compare nouns.

Add *–er* to most adjectives to compare two people, places, or things.

Add *–est* to most adjectives to compare more than two people, places, or things.

> **Circle the correct form of the adjective that compares nouns.**

1. Anna is (taller, tallest) than Mark.

2. Jim's book is the (longest, longer) book in the collection.

3. His jersey is the (dirtier, dirtiest) of any player on the team!

4. Dean makes the (deliciousest, most delicious) meals.

5. The black bowling ball is (heaviest, heavier) than the blue ball.

> **Revisit a piece of your writing. Edit the draft to make sure all adjectives are used correctly.**

Connect to Writing: Using Adjectives That Compare

▶ **Read the selection and choose the best answer to each question.**

Martha wrote the following paragraph describing different animals at the zoo. Read her paragraph and look for revisions she should make. Then answer the questions that follow.

(1) We went to the newer zoo this weekend. (2) Elephants are the big animals at the zoo. (3) On the hottest days, the animals stay inside. (4) The snakes are slimiest than the birds. (5) The peacocks have the more interesting feathers.

1. Which statement below uses the comparative or superlative adjective properly?

   A. Elephants are the big animals at the zoo.

   B. On the hottest days, the animals stay inside.

   C. The snakes are slimiest than the birds.

   D. The peacocks have the more interesting feathers.

2. Which statement below is a properly edited version of statement 5?

   A. The peacocks have the more interesting feathers.

   B. The peacocks have the interestingest feathers.

   C. The peacocks have the most interestinger feathers.

   D. The peacocks have the most interesting feathers.

▶ **What is your favorite zoo animal? Write two or three sentences about it. Use adjectives to compare.**

_____

_____

_____

Adverbs That Tell How

> Words that describe verbs are called **adverbs**.
>
> Adverbs can tell how an action happens. Most adverbs that tell how end in *–ly*.
>
> Adverbs can come before or after the verbs they describe.
>
> She walked <u>slowly</u> across the bridge.
>
> The artist <u>carefully</u> painted a line across the canvas.

▶ **Write the adverb that tells about the underlined verb in each sentence.**

1. She <u>held</u> the balloon's string tightly. __tightly__

2. The boys cautiously <u>approached</u> the basement door. __cautiously__

3. Marlis proudly <u>showed</u> us her swimming trophy. __proudly__

4. Jamie gracefully <u>skated</u> across the ice. __gracefully__

5. The dog <u>gobbled</u> up his food hungrily. _____

6. We <u>spoke</u> quietly in the library. _____

7. The frog <u>leaped</u> suddenly into the pond. _____

8. The children <u>ran</u> quickly to the finish line. _____

9. We <u>spoke</u> happily about the trip. _____

10. The dog <u>barked</u> angrily at the cars. _____

▶ **Revisit a piece of your writing. Edit the draft to make sure that all adverbs that tell how are written correctly.**

Name _____

Adverbs That Tell Where and When

> **Adverbs** can tell how an action happens. They can also tell where and when something happens.
>
> Adverbs can come before or after the verbs they describe.
>
> I eat a big breakfast <u>daily</u>. (when)
>
> We brought the boxes <u>outside</u>. (where)

▸ **Write the adverb that tells about each underlined verb.**

1. First, we will <u>ask</u> our teacher for help. ___first___

2. You can <u>walk</u> behind me. ___behind___

3. Finally we <u>reached</u> the skate park. ___Finally___

4. Do not <u>look</u> down! _____

5. There will be a car <u>waiting</u> nearby. _____

6. I have never <u>skied</u> down a mountain. _____

7. Jasper <u>plays</u> softball weekly. _____

8. I will <u>write</u> that report soon. _____

9. The menu is <u>changed</u> daily. _____

10. Let's <u>bring</u> the toys inside before it rains. _____

▸ **Revisit a piece of your writing. Edit the draft to make sure that all adverbs that tell where and when are written correctly.**

Adverbs That Tell How, Where, and When

Words that describe verbs are **adverbs**. Adverbs can tell how, where, or when an actions happens. Adverbs can come before or after the verbs they describe.

> **Write the adverb that tells how the underlined verb happened.**

1. The ocean waves <u>roared</u> loudly on the beach.   ___loudly___

2. The crowd <u>cheered</u> excitedly for the team.   ___excitedly___

3. My dog <u>looked</u> at me quizzically.   ___quizzically___

4. The child <u>turned</u> in bed restlessly.   ___restlessly___

5. She <u>spoke</u> on the phone quietly.   ___quietly___

> **Write the adverb that tells where or when the underlined verb happened.**

6. We <u>ran</u> upstairs to the attic.   ___upstairs___

7. Are you going to <u>let</u> the cat inside?   ___going___

8. My grandparents <u>arrive</u> tomorrow.   ___tomorrow___

9. After <u>running</u>, I always need a lot of water.   _____

10. Let's <u>buy</u> the hat before it is sold out.   _____

> **Revisit a piece of your writing. Edit the draft to make sure that all adverbs that tell how, where, and when are written correctly.**

Review Adverbs

An **adverb** is a word that describes a verb. Adverbs can come before or after the verb they are describing. Adverbs tell how, when, and where an action happens.

Adverb That Tells How	Adverb That Tells When	Adverb That Tells Where
Ramon quietly walked into the room.	We need to sweep this floor daily.	I heard a noise outside.

▶ **Circle the adverb that describes the underlined verb. On the line, write** *how, when,* **or** *where* **to tell what the adverb tells about the verb.**

1. The boy <u>slurped</u> the soup noisily. _____

2. Janice <u>sang</u> yesterday in the choir. _____

3. Let's <u>run</u> back inside. _____

4. The dancer <u>spun</u> gracefully across the stage. _____

5. We will <u>watch</u> a new show tomorrow. _____

6. The girl <u>drew</u> a straight line carefully. _____

7. He <u>smiled</u> cheerfully at me. _____

8. Lionel always <u>likes</u> dessert. _____

9. They must <u>water</u> the plant frequently. _____

10. We quickly <u>sold</u> out of the cookies at the bake sale. _____

▶ **Revisit a piece of your writing. Edit the draft to make sure that all adverbs are written correctly.**

Connect to Writing: Using Adverbs

> **Read the selection and choose the best answer to each question.**

Read the following paragraph about two boys walking home. Look for any revisions that should be made. Then answer the questions that follow.

(1) Gavin and Reese were on their way home from school. (2) Gavin was walking very quickly. (3) Reese was walking slow behind him. (4) Gavin turned around sharply to see what was taking Reese so long. (5) Reese was looking at the ground careful. (6) There was a slug making its way across the road. (7) Reese asked Gavin if he had ever seen anything move so slowly. (8) Gavin grinned and nodded thoughtfully.

1. Which of these statements uses an adverb incorrectly?

   A. Gavin and Reese were walking home from school.

   B. Gavin was walking very quickly.

   C. Reese was walking slow behind him.

   D. Gavin turned around sharply to see what was taking Reese so long.

2. Which of these statements uses an adverb incorrectly?

   A. Reese was looking at the ground careful.

   B. There was a slug making its way across the road.

   C. Reese asked Gavin if he had ever seen anything move so slowly.

   D. Gavin grinned and nodded thoughtfully.

> **How do you like to walk—quickly or slowly? Write two or three sentences to tell why.**

_____

_____

_____

Adverbs That Compare

> **Adverbs** can tell where, when, or how something happens. Adverbs are used to describe verbs. Adverbs can also be used to compare actions.
>
> To compare two actions, use the ending *-er* with most adverbs, such as *hard, late,* or *slow.*
>
> Use *more* before adverbs that end in *-ly,* such as *carefully* or *quickly.*
>
> I run <u>slower</u> than you.
>
> You write <u>more carefully</u> than I do.

▶ **Choose the correct adverb in parentheses. Write it on the line.**

1. She was walking (rapidly, more rapidly) than I was. _____

2. The bus stopped (abruptly, more abruptly) than we expected.

   _____

3. The ballerina danced (longer, more long) in this performance.

   _____

4. Jeremy acts (seriously, more seriously) than his older brother.

   _____

5. Cassie smiled (warmly, more warmly) than the others.

   _____

▶ **Revisit a piece of your writing. Edit the draft to make sure that all adverbs are written correctly.**

Adverbs That Compare Two Actions

Adverbs can be used to compare two actions.

Add *-er* to one-syllable adverbs to show comparison. If the adverb ends with *e*, drop the *e* before adding *-er*.

Use *more* before adverbs that end in *-ly*. Sometimes, an adverb that ends with *-ly* will use an *-ier* ending.

> The sun shines <u>brighter</u> than other stars.

> We woke up <u>later</u> on the weekend.

> That green jacket looks <u>fancier</u> than the red one.

> Write the correct form of the adverb in parentheses to complete the sentence.

1. Emily arrived (early) than we expected. _____

2. The train travels (quickly) than the bus. _____

3. Tracy dances (gracefully) than her sister. _____

4. We will need to climb (high) to reach the top. _____

5. I swim (fast) than I did last year. _____

> Revisit a piece of your writing. Edit the draft to make sure that all adverbs are written correctly.

Adverbs That Compare More Than Two Actions

When adverbs are used to compare more than two actions, add –est.

For adverbs that end in –y, change the y to i.

For adverbs that end in –ly, use most to compare more than two actions.

▷ **Write the correct form of the adverb that compares more than two actions.**

1. eagerly _____

2. furiously _____

3. late _____

4. perfectly _____

5. patiently _____

6. high _____

▷ **Write the form of the adverb that compares more than two actions.**

7. Russ walked _____ of all the hikers. (slowly)

8. Andre ran the _____ of all the children. (quickly)

9. Christina worked the _____ of everyone in the group. (hard)

10. I woke up _____ on the days I had school. (early)

▷ **Revisit a piece of your writing. Edit the draft to make sure that all adverbs are written correctly.**

Review Adverbs That Compare

Adverbs tell when, where, or how something happened. They can also be used to compare actions.

Add the ending *–er* to adverbs to compare two actions.

To compare more than two actions, add the ending *–est*.

Adverb	Comparing Two Actions	Comparing More Than Two Actions
late	later	latest
quickly	more quickly	most quickly

Gary ran <u>fast</u>. Rachel ran <u>faster</u> than Gary. Manny ran <u>fastest</u> of all.

▶ **Write the correct form of the adverb in parentheses.**

1. Our dog Lola can run (fast) than our neighbor's dog. _____

2. Of the three of us, Elena sings the (loud). _____

3. Veronica writes (neatly) than Roberta. _____

4. Nate dove the (deep) of all the swimmers. _____

5. It will be (safe) to take the car than to walk. _____

▶ **Revisit a piece of your writing. Edit the draft to make sure that your adverbs are written correctly.**

Connect to Writing: Using Adverbs That Compare

> **Read the selection and choose the best answer to each question.**

Read the following paragraph about a race. Look for any revisions that should be made. Then answer the questions that follow.

(1) Eddie, Karen, and I had a race to see who ran faster. (2) Eddie was in the lead at first. (3) But Karen worked hard and soon ran past him. (4) I was slow, but I think I ran the most gracefully. (5) In the end, Karen won the race.

1. What change should be made to sentence 1?

   A. Change *faster* to *most fast*.

   B. Change *faster* to *more fast*.

   C. Change *faster* to *fastest*.

   D. Make no change.

2. What change should be made to sentence 4?

   A. Change *most gracefully* to *more gracefully*.

   B. Change *most gracefully* to *gracefuller*.

   C. Change *most gracefully* to *gracefullest*.

   D. Make no change.

> **Write two or three sentences about a race you have been in.**

_____

_____

_____

Adjectives That Compare

Adjectives are used to describe nouns. Adjectives can also be used to compare two or more nouns.

Add the ending –er to most adjectives to compare two nouns. Add –est to compare more than two nouns.

Adjective	Comparing Two Nouns	Comparing More Than Two Nouns
tall	taller	tallest
high	higher	highest
large	larger	largest

Monica is tall. Dana is taller than Monica. Jessie is tallest of all.

> **Write the correct form of the adjective in parentheses.**

1. I am a (fast) runner than my little brother. _____

2. That one is the (bright) star in the sky tonight. _____

3. The (small) kitten in the litter was the white one. _____

4. The sand near the water is (cool) than the sand further out.

_____

5. The book's first chapter is (long) than the second chapter.

_____

> **Revisit a piece of your writing. Edit the draft to make sure that you use adjectives that compare correctly.**

Adverbs That Compare

Adverbs tell when, where, or how something happened. They can also be used to compare actions. Add the ending –er to adverbs to compare two actions. When the adverb ends in –ly place the word more or most in front of the adverb. To compare more than two actions, add the ending –est.

Adverb	Comparing Two Actions	Comparing More Than Two Actions
fast	faster	fastest
quickly	more quickly	most quickly

Kyle ran fast. Cassie ran faster than Kyle. Rosa ran the fastest of all.

▶ **Write the correct form of the adverb in parentheses.**

1. Eva and I climbed high in the tree, but Carlos climbed (high).

   _____

2. Jason grew to be the (tall) boy in our class. _____

3. We talked (quietly) in the library than we usually do. _____

4. The new submarine dives (deep) than the old one. _____

5. The audience clapped (hard) for Max than for anyone else.

   _____

▶ **Revisit a piece of your writing. Edit the draft to make sure all adverbs that compare are used correctly.**

Using Adjectives and Adverbs

> Adjectives compare nouns.
>
> Adverbs compare verbs, or actions.

> **Write an adjective or adverb to complete each sentence. Then write**
> *adjective* **or** *adverb* **to identify the answer you gave.**

1. George swings _____ . (quiet) _____

2. Locusts are the _____ of all insects. (hungry)

   _____

3. The waves splashed _____ than they had earlier in the day.

   (high) _____

4. The waters near the Arctic are _____ than the waters near

   Mexico. (cold) _____

> **Write three sentences. Include an adjective that compares in two**
> **sentences and an adverb that compares in the other sentence.**

5. _____

6. _____

7. _____

> **Revisit a piece of your writing. Edit the draft to make sure all adjectives**
> **and adverbs that compare are used correctly.**

Review Adjectives and Adverbs
That Compare

Use *−er* and *more* to compare two nouns. Use *−est* and *most* to compare three or more nouns.

Add *−er* or *−est* to most adjectives that have one syllable.

Add *more* or *most* before adjectives that have three or more syllables.

Use *−er* or *more* to compare two verbs, or actions. Use *−est* or *most* to compare three or more.

Add *−er* or *−est* to most adverbs that have one syllable.

Add *more* or *most* before adverbs that end in *−ly*.

> **Write the correct form of the adjective or adverb in parentheses.**

1. My suitcase is (light) than yours. _____

2. This science test is the (easy) one I ever took. _____

3. Yesterday's storm was (powerful) than the one last week.

 _____

4. The wind is blowing (quietly) than it was earlier. _____

5. My old shoes are (tight) than my new ones. _____

> **Revisit a piece of your writing. Edit the draft to make sure all adjectives and adverbs that compare are used correctly.**

Connect to Writing: Using Adjectives and Adverbs That Compare

▶ **Read the selection and choose the best answer to each question.**

Read the following paragraph about a boy who is very hungry after a hike. Look for any revisions that should be made. Then answer the questions that follow.

(1) Harry spent an entire day hiking with his family. (2) When he got home, he was hungrier than he had ever been before. (3) He saw a plate of brownies on the kitchen table. (4) He greedily gobbled down four brownies. (5) They were the more delicious brownies he'd ever had!

1. What change should be made to sentence 2?

    A. *Hungrier* should be *hungriest*.

    B. *Hungrier* should be *more hungry*.

    C. *Hungrier* should be *most hungry*.

    D. Make no change.

2. What change should be made to sentence 5?

    A. *More delicious* should be *deliciousest*.

    B. *More delicious* should be *deliciouser*.

    C. *More delicious* should be *most delicious*.

    D. Make no change.

▶ **What food do you like to eat when you are very hungry? Write two or three sentences about it.**

_____

_____

_____

Introduce Prepositions

A **preposition** shows the connection between words in a
sentence. Some prepositions describe time. Others describe place.

Common Prepositions					
about	at	down	inside	out	under
above	before	during	into	outside	until
across	behind	except	near	over	up
after	below	for	of	past	with
along	beside	from	off	through	without
around	by	in	on	to	

> **Underline the preposition in each sentence.**

1. Please do not talk during the movie.

2. This book is about dinosaurs.

3. My best friend Sheila lives across the street.

4. Our cat Pepper likes to hide under the couch.

5. What do you think is inside the large box?

> **Revisit a piece of your writing. Edit the draft to make sure all prepositions
are used correctly.**

Prepositional Phrases

A **prepositional phrase** begins with a preposition and ends with a noun or a pronoun. Both these words and all of the words in between them make up the prepositional phrase.

The ball rolled **down** the hill.

> Underline the prepositional phrase in each sentence.

1. Please place the forks and knives on the table.

2. You will not receive my gift until next week.

3. After a few minutes we realized Jessie wasn't home.

4. We sat beside the river and had a picnic.

5. By the evening, we were too tired to see the movie.

6. You should come over after school.

7. My great aunt from Ohio is 84.

8. We can take a walk before dinner.

9. The dog followed her down the stairs.

10. Bring the groceries into the kitchen.

> Revisit a piece of your writing. Edit the draft to make sure all prepositions are used correctly.

Prepositional Phrases That Tell When and Where

Some prepositional phrases tell **when**, and start with words such as *before, after,* or *during*. Others tell **where**, and start with words such *over, in, on, above,* or *below*.

> We can have those brownies <u>after dinner</u>.
>
> I think Judy is <u>in the next room</u>.

▸ **Underline the prepositional phrase that tells *when*.**

1. During the play, Hilary sang a solo.

2. Can you meet me before five o'clock?

3. After breakfast, I will wash the dishes.

4. It was completely quiet after the storm.

5. Don't go outside during the storm.

▸ **Underline the prepositional phrase that tells *where*.**

6. Kenny jumped over the wall and ran away.

7. Lyle hung a picture above his desk.

8. Please read the paragraph below the title.

9. The cupcakes in the oven are ready now.

10. The sale items are located throughout the store.

▸ **Revisit a piece of your writing. Edit the draft to make sure all prepositions are used correctly.**

Review Prepositions and Prepositional Phrases

Prepositions	Prepositional Phrases
from	Louise walked from her house.
to	Louise walked to the store.

▶ Circle the preposition and underline the rest of the prepositional phrase in each sentence.

1. The present in the biggest box is mine.

2. Blondie is hiding under the bed.

3. I prefer the dress with the gold belt.

4. Rebecca and Mark are in the kitchen.

5. After dinner, let's play a game.

6. The cake on the kitchen table is still cooling.

7. These earrings were a gift from my grandmother.

8. The broom is behind the back door.

9. She held the umbrella high over our heads.

10. Some of the food fell under the table.

▶ Revisit a piece of your writing. Edit the draft to make sure all prepositions and prepositional phrases are used correctly.

Connect to Writing: Combining Sentences Using Prepositional Phrases

> **Read the selection and choose the best answer to each question.**

Read the following paragraph about going to the dentist. Look for any revisions that should be made. Then answer the questions that follow.

(1) On Friday morning, Mitchell went to the dentist. (2) He was going for a check-up, and he was a little worried. (3) The dentist checked beside his mouth. (4) He did not find any cavities. (5) Soon the check-up was over. (6) The dentist handed Mitchell a tiny airplane toy. (7) Finally, Mitchell smiled.

1. What change should be made to sentence 1?

   A. Change *on* to *by*.

   B. Change *on* to *before*.

   C. Change *on* to *after*.

   D. Make no change.

2. What change should be made to sentence 3?

   A. Change *beside* to *outside*.

   B. Change *beside* to *below*.

   C. Change *beside* to *inside*.

   D. Make no change.

> **How do you feel about going to the dentist? Write two or three sentences about it.**

_____

_____

_____

Commas in a Series of Nouns

A **series** is a list of three or more words used in a sentence. Use commas to separate three or more nouns included in a series. Commas tell readers when to pause.

This salad has lettuce, tomatoes, and cucumbers.

> **Write each sentence correctly. Add commas where they are needed.**

1. Rachel Miguel and I are in the same class.

   _____

2. We have swim lessons on Mondays Wednesdays and Thursdays.

   _____

3. My favorite ice cream flavors are chocolate strawberry and coconut.

   _____

4. The colors of this flag are red white and green.

   _____

5. The dance school offers classes in jazz tap and ballet.

   _____

> **Revisit a piece of your writing. Edit the draft to make sure commas in a series of nouns are used correctly.**

Commas in a Series of Verbs

A **series** is a list of three or more words used in a sentence. Use commas to separate three or more verbs included in a series. Commas tell readers when to pause.

Luca planted, watered, and harvested the green beans.

> **Write each sentence correctly. Add commas where they are needed.**

1. The athletes in a triathlon must run bike and swim.

_____

2. The cat yawned stretched and licked its paw.

_____

3. During the play, the audience clapped stomped and laughed.

_____

4. The ballerina danced leapt and twirled.

_____

5. We dug raked and planted seeds in the garden.

_____

> **Revisit a piece of your writing. Edit the draft to make sure all commas in a series of verbs are used correctly.**

Commas in Addresses

> Use a comma to separate each part of an address.
>
> Suzannah Crosby, 87 Willow Street, Detroit, Michigan

▶ **Write each address correctly. Add commas where they are needed.**

1. Andrew Berman 892 West 13th Street New York New York

_____

2. Veronica Frascatti 43 Maiden Lane Oscola Florida

_____

3. The package needs to be delivered to Diana Hernandez 788 Firewood Avenue Castle New Mexico.

_____

_____

4. My friend lives at 566 Chestnut Street Nashua New Hampshire.

_____

5. We are moving to 79 Kentucky Avenue Billings Montana.

_____

▶ **Revisit a piece of your writing. Edit the draft to make sure all commas in addresses are used correctly.**

Review Commas

A **series** is a list of three or more words used in a sentence. Use commas to separate three or more nouns or verbs included in a series. Commas tell readers when to pause.

We found marbles, jacks, and coins in the attic.

Use a comma to separate each part of an address.

Victoria O'Hanlon, 56 West End Drive, Louisville, Kentucky

▷ **Write each sentence correctly. Add commas where they are needed.**

1. Please send this letter to Callie Barlow 548 Myrtle Avenue Rochester New York.

_____

2. My friends and I were swimming diving and jumping off the dock.

_____

3. We picked blueberries strawberries and peaches this summer.

_____

4. The Wrigleys have cows pigs and goats on their farm.

_____

5. I live at 8979 Richmond Street Amarillo Texas.

_____

▷ **Revisit a piece of your writing. Edit the draft to make sure all commas are used correctly.**

Connect to Writing: Using Commas

> **Read the selection and choose the best answer to each question.**

Read the following paragraph about writing a letter. Look for any revisions that should be made. Then answer the questions that follow.

(1) Lena is writing a letter to her grandmother. (2) She tells her all about what she is learning in school. (3) She tells her that her favorite subjects are math reading, and science. (4) She talks about what they will do together when her grandmother visits again. (5) Finally, Lena is done with the letter. (6) She puts the letter in an envelope. (7) She addresses the envelope to Mrs. Joan Glass, 1718 Woodsman Street, Baltimore Maryland. (8) Then she puts the letter in the mail.

1. What change should be made to sentence 3?

   A. There should be a comma after *math*.

   B. There should be a comma after *subjects*.

   C. There should be a comma after *are*.

   D. Make no change.

2. What change should be made to sentence 7?

   A. There should be a comma after *Woodsman*.

   B. There should be a comma after *Baltimore*.

   C. There should be a comma after *1718*.

   D. Make no change.

> **Who would you like to write a letter to? Write two or three sentences to tell why and what you would like to write.**

_____

_____

_____

Commas in a Series

A **series** is a list of three or more words together in a sentence.

Use a comma to separate the words in a series.

It was hot, dry, and windy in the desert.

> **Rewrite each sentence correctly. Add commas where they are needed.**

1. The balloons are red green and blue.

_____

2. Sara James and Bob are on the track team.

_____

3. Please buy eggs milk and butter at the store.

_____

4. Don't forget your hat gloves and scarf.

_____

5. I have vacations in September May and August

_____

> **Revisit a piece of your writing. Edit the draft to make sure all commas in a series are used correctly.**

_____

_____

Introductory Words

Use a comma after the introductory words *well, yes,* and *no.*

Use a comma after order words such as *first, second, next,* and *finally.*

Do not use a comma after *then.*

Yes, I'd like to go to the concert.

> **Rewrite each sentence correctly. Add commas where they are needed.**

1. First I have to finish my homework.

First, I have to finish my homework.

2. Then I can go to the playground.

Then, I can go to the playground.

3. Well I guess I can help you.

Well, I guess I can help you.

4. Finally bake the cake.

Finally, Bak the cake.

5. Yes I told him we were leaving.

Yes, I told him we were leaving.

> **Revisit a piece of your writing. Edit the draft to make sure commas after introductory words are used correctly.**

Commas in Sentences

Commas are used in a date or when listing city and state in a sentence.

Commas are also used when combining sentences and when using nouns or verbs in a series.

On July 4, 1976, in Washington, DC, there were parties, fireworks, and picnics.

> **Rewrite each sentence with a comma where it belongs in a date or a place.**

1. John was born on February 3 2008.

   _____

2. We are going to Orlando Florida for vacation.

   _____

3. The library will be closed on Sunday November 20.

   _____

> **Combine each group of sentences. Put the nouns or verbs in a series with commas. Write the new sentence.**

4. The circus had clowns. The circus had lions. The circus had acrobats.

   _____

5. The car was packed. The van was packed. The trailer was packed.

   _____

> **Revisit a piece of your writing. Edit the draft to make sure all commas are used correctly.**

_____

Grade 3 • Commas in Sentences and in Series

Review Commas in Sentences and in Series

Commas are used in a date or when listing city and state in a sentence.

Commas are also used when combining sentences and when using nouns or verbs in a series.

Also use a comma to separate an introductory word like *first, next,* or *finally.* Do not use a comma after *then.*

> The party is on January 28, 2018 in San Diego, California.

> We need to buy cookies, crackers, and cheese for the party.

> Finally, we need to make sure we arrive on time.

▶ **Insert a comma where it belongs in the sentences below.**

1. James is coming for a visit on October 12 2019.

2. My sister was born in Silver Spring Maryland.

3. My favorite colors are red blue and yellow.

4. First tell everyone where you are from.

5. Next tell us how to spell your name.

▶ **Revisit a piece of your writing. Edit the draft to make sure all commas are used correctly.**

Grade 3 • Commas in Sentences and in Series

Printable
129

Connect to Writing: Using Commas in Sentences and in Series

> **Read the selection and choose the best answer to each question.**

John wrote the following paragraph about his baseball team's spring season. Read his paragraph and look for revisions he should make. Then answer the questions that follow.

(1) We had a winning baseball team this year, with Jake Laura and Sally. (2) We played on Tuesday evenings. (3) First we set out the bases on the diamond. (4) After practice, we put away the bats gloves and batting helmets. (5) Dylan Frannie and Mia are going to join the team next year.

1. Which statement below uses commas properly?

    A. We had a winning baseball team this year, with Jake Laura and Sally.

    B. First we set out the bases on the diamond.

    C. After practice, we put away the bats, gloves, and batting helmets.

    D. Dylan Frannie and Mia are going to join the team next year.

2. Which statement below is a properly edited version of statement 5?

    A. Dylan Frannie and, Mia are going to join the team next year.

    B. Dylan, Frannie and Mia are going to join the team next year.

    C. Dylan, Frannie, and Mia are going to join the team next year.

    D. Dylan, Frannie, and Mia, are going to join the team next year.

> **What sports do you play or want to play? Write two or three sentences about it.**

_____

_____

_____

Quotation Marks

> **Quotation marks** (" ") show dialogue, or the exact words a person or character says.
>
> Put quotation marks at the beginning and the end of a person's or character's exact words.
>
> Sam said, "I plan to grow vegetables."

▷ Rewrite the sentences, adding quotation marks as needed.

1. Sam said, It's time to buy seeds.

sam said(its time to buy seeds)

2. The soil is starting to warm up, said Mom.

The soil is(starting to warm up said mom)

3. Pretty soon it will be summer, said Jack.

pretty soon(it will be summer said jack)

4. When will the bean seeds sprout? asked Sarah.

when will the (bean seeds sprout?asked sara

5. Mom replied, As soon as the weather warms up.

Mom Replied(as soon as the weather warms up)

▷ Revisit a piece of your writing. Edit the draft to make sure you are using quotation marks correctly.

Capitalizing and Punctuating Quotations

Always capitalize the first word of the speaker's exact words.

If the quotation comes first, add a comma, question mark, or exclamation point inside the quotation marks at the end of the speaker's words and add a period at the end of the sentence.

If the quotation comes last, add a comma at the end of the tag and a question mark, exclamation point, or period inside the quotation marks.

> **Rewrite the sentences with correct capitalization and punctuation.**

1. Sam exclaimed "my garden is growing fast"

   _____

2. Mom said "we can sell those vegetables at the farm stand"

   _____

3. "we have three kinds of melons" Sam said

   _____

4. "how will we transport the vegetables to the market" Sarah asked

   _____

5. "we can use Dad's truck" Mom said

   _____

> **Revisit a piece of your writing. Edit the draft to make sure you are capitalizing and punctuating quotations correctly.**

Commas in Quotations

Use a comma to separate a quotation from explanations anywhere else in the same sentence.

"I like to eat vegetables," said Skylar.

Spencer said, "I like to eat fruit."

"I like both fruit and vegetables," said Shane, "but I prefer fruit."

▷ **Rewrite the sentences using correct capitalization and punctuation.**

1. "that painting is beautiful" Jane said

   _____

2. Mom asked "did you do it in art class"

   _____

3. "yes" Jane said

   _____

4. She explained "we studied modern art"

   _____

5. "Then we made our own masterpieces" Jane said

   _____

▷ **Revisit a piece of your writing. Edit the draft to make sure you are capitalizing and punctuating quotations correctly.**

Writing Quotations

Show dialogue by putting quotation marks (" ") at the beginning and the end of a speaker's exact words.

Place a comma after *said* or *asked* when it comes before the quoted words. Use a capital letter for the first word of the quotation and an end mark inside the quotation marks.

"Yes," Mark said.   Mariel said, "I'm feeling much better."

▶ **Write each sentence correctly. Use quotation marks, correct capitalization, end marks, and punctuation.**

1. The principal said, please do not run in the halls.

_____

2. Jane said I don't know the rules.

_____

3. Running inside is dangerous Jim explained.

_____

4. Jasper asked would you like to play after school

_____

5. I can't today I said.

_____

▶ **Revisit a piece of your writing. Edit the draft to make sure you are using quotation marks, capitalization, and punctuation correctly.**

Connect to Writing: Using Quotations

▶ **Read the selection and choose the best answer to each question.**

Jasper wrote the following paragraph about cooking spaghetti for dinner. Read his paragraph and look for revisions he should make. Then answer the questions that follow.

(1) What are you making for dinner asked Sarah. (2) Harry said I'm making spaghetti. (3) "Do you like spaghetti"? Harry asked. (4) Sarah said I love spaghetti. (5) "Everyone loves spaghetti!" said Harry.

1. Which statement does not contain an error?

A. What are you making for dinner asked Sarah.

B. Harry said I'm making spaghetti.

C. "Do you like spaghetti"? Harry asked.

D. "Everyone loves spaghetti!" said Harry.

2. Which statement below is a properly edited version of statement 3?

A. "Do you like spaghetti"? Harry asked.

B. Do you like spaghetti? Harry asked.

C. "Do you like spaghetti?" Harry asked.

D. "Do you like spaghetti" Harry asked?

▶ **What is your favorite dinner? Write two or three sentences about it.**

_____

_____

_____

Contractions with *Not*

You can put together two words and make a **contraction**. An apostrophe (')
takes the place of any letter or letters that are left out. Many contractions
combine a verb with *not*. The contraction *won't* is special. You form it from the
words *will not* and change the spelling.

It is not easy being the new kid in class.
It isn't easy being the new kid in class. (combine *is* and *not* into *isn't*)

Ben was not afraid to make new friends.
Ben wasn't afraid to make new friends. (combine *was* and *not* into *wasn't*)

▶ **Write the contraction for the words in parentheses.**

1. Gardens ___don't___ grow without sunlight. (do not)

2. James ___doesn't___ like to dig in the dirt. (does not)

3. Sarah ___won't___ help with the garden if she sees a worm. (will not)

4. We ___weren't___ aware that it was going to rain. (were not)

5. The soil ___wouldn't___ have been workable if it had rained. (would not)

6. Jack ___hasn't___ put the fence up around the garden. (has not)

7. The rabbits ___can't___ enter the garden. (cannot)

8. I ___couldn't___ have planted the garden without your help. (could not)

9. The garden ___won't___ grow without rain. (will not)

10. The rabbits ___can't___ get much to eat. (cannot)

▶ **Revisit a piece of your writing. Edit the draft to make sure that you are
writing contractions with *not* correctly.**

Contractions with Pronouns

You can put a pronoun and a verb together to make a **contraction**. An apostrophe replaces the letter or letters that are left out.

He says that he is on vacation.
He says that <u>he's</u> on vacation. (combine *he* and *is*)

We will see if the weather is nice.
<u>We'll</u> see if the weather is nice. (combine *we* and *will*)

▶ **Write the contraction for the words in parentheses.**

1. _____ be fun to go snorkeling. (It will)

2. _____ read a lot about coral reefs. (We have)

3. Make sure _____ ready to jump in the water. (you are)

4. _____ going to be the first one in. (I am)

5. _____ tell us when it is time to get out. (They will)

6. _____ going to be a beautiful day. (It is)

7. _____ seen almost the entire reef. (We have)

8. She says _____ come back again next year. (she will)

9. They want to see how _____ doing. (you are)

10. We think _____ call when it is time to snorkel. (they will)

▶ **Revisit a piece of your writing. Edit the draft to make sure that you are writing contractions with pronouns correctly.**

Contractions with *Not* and Pronouns

You can put together two words and make a **contraction**. An apostrophe
(') takes the place of any letter or letters that are left out. Many
contractions combine a verb with *not*. The contraction *won't* is special.
You form it from the words *will not* and change the spelling.

You can put a pronoun and a verb together to make a contraction. An
apostrophe replaces the letter or letters that are left out.

We are spending the day at the water park.
<u>We're</u> spending the day at the water park. (combine *we* and *are*)

She will get a sunburn without sunscreen.
<u>She'll</u> get a sunburn without sunscreen. (combine *she* and *will*)

> **Write the contraction for the words in parentheses.**

1. We _haven't_ been skiing in a long time. (have not)

2. We _didn't_ think it would be a hard sport. (did not)

3. Make sure _you'r_ wearing your helmet! (you are)

4. _I'm_ going to be the first one down the hill. (I am)

5. _They'll_ tell us when it the lifts are about to close. (They will)

6. _you'r_ going to love skiing. (You are)

7. _We've_ been to this mountain three times. (We have)

8. _She's_ an experienced skier. (She is)

9. _They've_ reported it will snow three feet tonight. (They have)

10. _We'll_ be happy to ski tomorrow if there is more snow. (We will)

Review Contractions with *Not* and Pronouns

You can put together two words and make a **contraction**. An apostrophe (') takes the place of any letter or letters that are left out. Many contractions combine a verb with *not*. The contraction *won't* is special. You form it from the words *will not* and change the spelling.

You can put a pronoun and a verb together to make a contraction. An apostrophe replaces the letter or letters that are left out.

I did not know you were born in Canada.
I <u>didn't</u> know you were born in Canada. (combine *did* and *not*)

They will go there on their way to camp.
<u>They'll</u> go there on their way to camp. (combine *they* and *will*)

> **Edit the following paragraph to use contractions for the underlined words and write it on the lines.**

At the end of the summer I <u>can not</u> wait to go back to school. I <u>do not</u> know why, but I get tired of summer vacation. <u>I will</u> talk to my friends, and <u>they will</u> understand! Sarah said <u>she is</u> anxious to go back to school.

_____

_____

_____

_____

> **Revisit a piece of your writing. Edit the draft to make sure that you are writing contractions with *not* and pronouns correctly.**

Connect to Writing: Forming Contractions Correctly

> **Read the selection and choose the best answer to each question.**

Sarah wrote the following paragraph about her school's Fall Festival. Read her paragraph and look for revisions she should make. Then answer the questions that follow.

     (1) Wer'e organizing a fall festival. (2) I ca'nt wait until the leaves start to fall and the air gets cool. (3) Last year I wa'snt here during the fall festival. (4) This year I'm going to make sure I can attend. (5) They've said it is fun.

1. Which statement below uses a contraction properly?

   A. Wer'e organizing a fall festival.

   B. I ca'nt wait until the leaves start to fall and the air gets cool.

   C. Last year I wa'snt here during the fall festival.

   D. This year I'm going to make sure I can attend.

2. Which statement below is a properly edited version of statement 5?

   A. They've said it is fun.

   B. Th'eyve said it is fun.

   C. Theyve said it is fun.

   D. Theyv'e said it is fun.

> **What is your favorite fall activity? Write two or three sentences about it.**

_____

_____

_____

Days and Months

An **abbreviation** is a shortened form of a word. Most
abbreviations begin with a capital letter and end with a period.
The months May, June, and July are generally not abbreviated, but
are spelled out.

Friday; <u>Fri.</u>

October; <u>Oct.</u>

▶ **Write the correct abbreviation for each day and month.**

1. Sunday _____

2. July _____

3. February _____

4. Wednesday _____

5. August _____

6. Monday _____

7. January _____

8. Thursday _____

9. April _____

10. May _____

▶ **Revisit a piece of your writing. Edit the draft to make sure that you are
writing abbreviations correctly.**

Places

An **abbreviation** is a shortened form of a word.

Places with names that can be abbreviated include roads, streets, lanes, avenues, and boulevards.

Jasmine Rd., Oak St., East Ln., Stafford Ave., and Lincoln Blvd.

▶ **Write each place name correctly using abbreviations.**

1. High Street _____

2. Garrison Boulevard _____

3. North Oak Lane _____

4. Westchester Avenue _____

5. Maple Street _____

6. Ocean Avenue _____

7. Rock Court _____

8. Delta Drive _____

9. Bronson Avenue _____

10. Lester Lane _____

▶ **Revisit a piece of your writing. Edit the draft to make sure that you are writing abbreviations correctly.**

Writing Abbreviations

An **abbreviation** is a shortened form of a word.

Days and months can be abbreviated. Wednesday / <u>Wed.</u>, and October / <u>Oct.</u>

Places with names that can be abbreviated include roads, streets, lanes, avenues, and boulevards. Jasmine <u>Rd.</u>, Oak <u>St.</u>, East <u>Ln.</u>, Stafford <u>Ave.</u>, and Lincoln <u>Blvd.</u>

> **Write the correct abbreviation for each day and month.**

1. Friday _____ Fri.

2. August _____ Aug.

3. September _____ Sept.

4. Tuesday _____ Tues.

5. December _____ Dec.

> **Abbreviate each place name correctly.**

6. Main Street _____ Street.

7. Alba Lane _____ Lane.

8. Commerce Drive _____ Drive.

9. Broadway Boulevard _____ Boulevard.

10. Camilia Court _____ Court.

> **Revisit a piece of your writing. Edit the draft to make sure that you are writing abbreviations correctly.**

Review Abbreviations

Proofreading your work for correctly spelled abbreviations will make your writing stronger.

Incorrect Abbreviation	Correct Abbreviation
mon; feb	Mon.; Feb.
ave.; st.	Ave.; St.

▶ **Rewrite this informal letter using abbreviations correctly.**

Mon, jan 3
Mom and Dad,

I'm having a great time at camp since I arrived here last fri. I've met new friends, including Bob from Orlando and Will from Portland. Sarah lives down the street from us on Branch blvd We are going to meet up the sun after camp is over for a party at Jack's house on Main str.

Ben

_____

_____

_____

_____

▶ **Revisit a piece of your writing. Edit the draft to make sure that you are writing abbreviations correctly.**

_____

Connect to Writing: Using Abbreviations

▶ **Read the selection and choose the best answer to each question.**

James wrote the following paragraph about his family's summer vacation. Read his paragraph and look for revisions he should make. Then answer the questions that follow.

    (1) Last summer, on August 12 2017 my family went on a road trip. (2) We left on a Tuesday and came home the following Wednesday. (3) The trip was just over one week long, and we traveled 645 miles. (4) We visited the White House at 1600 Pennsylvania Avenue in Washington, District of Columbia. (5) It was a fun trip, but I was relieved to arrive back home at our house on 1305 Mayberry Boulevard.

1. Which statement below is a properly abbreviated and punctuated verison of statement 1?

    A. Last summer, on August 12, 2017, my family went on a road trip.

    B. Last summer, on Aug. 12 2017 my family went on a road trip.

    C. Last summer, on Aug. 12 2017, my family went on a road trip.

    D. Last summer, on Aug.12, 2017, my family went on a road trip.

2. Which statement below is a properly abbreviated verison of statement 4?

    A. We visited the White House at 1600 Pennsylvania Ave. in Washington, DC.

    B. We visited the White House at 1600 PA Ave. in WA, DC.

    C. We visited the White House at 1600 Pennsylvania Ave. in Washington, DC.

    D. We visited the White House at 1600 Pennsylvania Ave. in Washington, District of Columbia.

▶ **Have you ever been to Washington DC? Write about what you saw there, or what you would like to see there if you took a trip.**

_____

_____

Spelling Irregular Plurals

Nouns are often made plural by adding –s or –es.

Irregular plural nouns are nouns that have special plural forms.

Some nouns do not change between the singular and plural forms.

desk, desks (add –s to make *desk* plural)

mix, mixes (add –es to make *mix* plural)

child, children (*children* is the plural form of *child*)

deer, deer (*deer* does not change from singular to plural)

> **Determine the plural form of the singular nouns below.**

1. hat _____

2. box _____

3. dish _____

4. fish _____

5. goose _____

6. shelf _____

7. foot _____

8. man _____

9. baby _____

10. tooth _____

> **Revisit a piece of your writing. Edit the draft to make sure that you are spelling irregular plural nouns correctly.**

Spelling Irregular Verbs

Adding –d, –ed, –ied to a verb can describe an action that happened in the past.

Irregular verbs do not use the –d, –ed, or –ied ending to show past action.

Irregular verbs have a different spelling to show past action, and they have another spelling when used with *has, have,* or *had*.

> go, went, has gone   get, got, has gotten
>
> come, came, has come

▶ **Choose the proper form of the verb in parentheses.**

1. I had never (saw, seen) a black and white movie. _____

2. Dad (came, come) home late from work last night. _____

3. We had already (ate, eaten). _____

4. We (saw, seen) the sun set. _____

5. My, how you've (grew, grown)! _____

6. I have already (choosed, chosen) my dress for the party. _____

7. He (hanged, hung) up his coat in the closet. _____

8. She (shook, shaked) the milkshake to mix the flavors. _____

9. The boy (swimmed, swam) in the deep part of the lake. _____

10. The teacher (buyed, bought) snacks for the class today. _____

▶ **Revisit a piece of your writing. Edit the draft to make sure that you are spelling irregular verbs correctly.**

Spelling High-Frequency Words

> Some words appear more often than others. These words are high-frequency words.
>
> Some commonly used words are compound words.
>
> Some commonly used words are spelled differently than they sound.

▶ **Choose the proper form of the high-frequency word in parentheses.**

1. Her uniform looks (diferent, different). _____

2. I want (everything, everthing) on my pizza. _____

3. I learn (something, somthing) from every book I read. _____

4. She will (definitely, definately) be there. _____

5. That test was (impossible, imposible) _____

▶ **Revisit a piece of your writing. Edit the draft to make sure that you are spelling high-frequency words correctly.**

Review Spelling

Irregular plural nouns are nouns that do not use –s or –es in the plural form.

Some nouns do not change between the singular and plural forms.

Irregular verbs don't use –d, –ed, or –ied to show past action, and they have another spelling when used with *has, have,* or *had.*

Some commonly used words are spelled differently than they sound, and are frequently misspelled.

▷ **Write the plural form of the word.**

1. goose _____

2. fox _____

3. mouse _____

4. sheep _____

5. tooth _____

▷ **Determine the correct past form of the irregular verbs in the sentences below.**

6. Jonas (go, went) on vacation last week. _____

7. Marsha thinks she (get, got) something in the mail today. _____

8. The bird (eat, ate) all of the bird seed. _____

9. The airplane (flew, flown) over the ocean. _____

10. Sally (chose, chosen) the cherry lollipop. _____

▷ **Revisit a piece of your writing. Edit the draft to make sure that you are spelling irregular plural nouns and irregular verbs correctly.**

Connect to Writing: Using Correct Spelling

▣ **Read the selection and choose the best answer to each question.**

Jason wrote the following paragraph about a trip he took with Sarah to visit her grandmother. Read his paragraph and look for revisions he should make. Then answer the questions that follow.

(1) Sarah and I went on a walk to visit her grandmother. (2) On the way, we seen a group of fifteen goose. (3) They look like they had just ate. (4) They usally come up to you looking for food, but this time they didn't. (5) We bringed a carrot cake for Sarah's grandmother. (6) We were hoping we wouldn't run into any foxs on the way.

1. Which statement does not contain an error?

   A. Sarah and I went on a walk to visit her grandmother.

   B. On the way, we seen a group of fifteen goose.

   C. They look like they had just ate.

   D. We bringed a carrot cake for Sarah's grandmother.

2. Which statement below is a properly edited version of statement 2?

   A. On the way, we saw a group of fifteen goose.

   B. On the way, we saw a group of fifteen geese.

   C. On the way, we seen a group of fifteen geeses.

   D. On the way, we seen a group of fifteen geese.

▣ **Where do you like to take a walk? Write two or three sentences about it.**

_____

_____

_____